ACOUSTIC GUITAR GUIDES

ACOUSTIC GUITAR OWNER'S MANUAL

STRING LETTER PUBLISHING

Publisher: David A. Lusterman

Editorial Director: Jeffrey Pepper Rodgers

Editor: Simone Solondz

Designer: Gary Cribb

Production Coordinator: Christi Payne

Marketing Manager: Jen Fujimoto

Cover photographs, clockwise from top left: Takamine G-330S (photo by Rory Earnshaw), Steve Grimes archtop (photo by Rory Earnshaw), Rodriguez classical, and maple-top Ovation.

Photographs and Illustrations: Scott Blum, p. 29; Rory Earnshaw, pp. 62, 73, 90; Harry Fleishman, pp. 33, 34, 59, 60, 61; Frank Ford, pp. 35, 54, 65, 70, 72, 74, 75, 76, 77, 78, 79, 80, 81, 86, 91, 92, 93; Laura Haertling, pp. 25, 26, 28; Paul Haggard, p. 16; Tony Harrison, p. 7, bottom; Michael Hoover, p. 15; Darryl Kluskowski, p. 48; Chugrad McAndrews, p. 7, top; Barry Price, pp. 17, 18, 19, 22, 23, 56, 57, 65, 67, 68, 69, 71, 84; Janet Smith, pp. 37, 39; Taylor Guitars, pp. 40, 41, 43, 44, 45, 55, 85, 94.

Printed in the United States of America.

All rights reserved. This book was produced by String Letter Publishing, Inc.

PO Box 767, San Anselmo, California 94979-0767

(415) 485-6946; www.acousticguitar.com

Library of Congress Cataloging-in-Publication Data

Acoustic guitar owner's manual

      p. cm — (Acoustic guitar guides)

      Includes index

   ISBN 1-890490-21-0

    1. Guitar—Maintenance and repair. I. Series.

ML1015.G9 A37 2000

787.87'192'8—dc21

STRING LETTER PUBLISHING

contents

introduction

These are inspiring times to play the acoustic guitar. Not only is the instrument used in an endless variety of music around the world, but the guitars themselves—in all price ranges and in all shapes and sizes—sound and feel better than they ever have.

Clearly an acoustic guitar's simplicity is key to its universal appeal—just pick it up and play, no wires required—but the instruments themselves are far from simple. Their design is a delicate balance of elements and tensions, and the more you know about how they work and how they change over time, the more music and satisfaction you'll get out of them.

In the last few decades, a tremendous amount of information has become available for would-be guitar builders and repairers, but surprisingly little has been translated and shared with those who want to *play* their guitars rather than file their frets or reglue their braces. At *Acoustic Guitar* magazine, we've made it our mission to fill this gap by supplying reliable, easy-to-understand information written expressly to address players' needs, and those efforts culminate in this book.

In the *Acoustic Guitar Owner's Manual* we start at the beginning, helping you get acquainted with your instrument and laying to rest some pervasive guitar myths, then proceed through basic care, with chapters on such critical issues as humidity, choosing a case, and flying with your guitar. Next comes setup (adjustments that can be tackled at home if you're so inclined), common repairs, and pickup installation. The repair section does *not* show you how to do a neck reset in your basement; instead, it helps you understand what this procedure is and why it might (or might not) be needed. In other words, our aim is to make you a more savvy guitar owner *and* repair-shop customer.

Over the last ten years, we've fielded thousands of questions from *Acoustic Guitar* readers about their instruments, and throughout this book, you'll find Q&A sidebars that address the most persistent and perplexing ones. If you find yourself confused by any of the terminology used in these pages, be sure to read "An Acoustic Guitar Primer" in the opening section, and check out "A Complete Glossary of Acoustic Guitar Lingo" in the back.

You love your guitar and want it to last for a long, long time. Now you can ignore the dubious advice from well-meaning friends and anonymous "experts" on the Web and get the answers you need from the real experts.

Jeffrey Pepper Rodgers
Editor
Acoustic Guitar Magazine

about the authors

DICK BOAK

Dick Boak has worked at the Martin Guitar Co. in Nazareth, Pennsylvania, since 1976. Originally hired as a design draftsman, he has been a builder of prototypes, manager of the 1833 Shop, founder of *A Woodworker's Dream* (which evolved into *Guitarmaker's Connection*), and manager of Martin's in-house advertising department and print shop. In addition to his varied responsibilities at Martin, Boak was instrumental in founding ASIA (the Association of Stringed Instrument Artisans), edited and published ASIA's *Guitarmaker* magazine from 1989 to 1995, and organized many of ASIA's biannual symposiums.

WILLIAM R. CUMPIANO

William R. Cumpiano was born in Puerto Rico 50 years ago and has been making guitars in the American, European, and Latin American traditions for more than 30 years. He builds his guitars by hand, one and two at a time, in his Northampton, Massachusetts, studio. He also teaches his craft and writes about his field in books, magazines, and on the Web at www.cumpiano.com. He is coauthor of the premier textbook in the field, *Guitarmaking: Tradition and Technology,* and is currently working on a new textbook about the myriad stringed instrument traditions of the U.S., Caribbean, and Central and South America.

HARRY FLEISHMAN

Harry Fleishman has been a custom guitar builder for more than 25 years. In his Boulder, Colorado, shop, he produces about a dozen guitars and basses annually and writes about guitars and lutherie-related issues for *Acoustic Guitar, Bass Frontier,* and *American Lutherie* magazines. He also teaches guitar making and is director at the American School of Lutherie, exhibits regularly at the Healdsburg Guitar Festival, and has lectured at Guild of American Luthiers conventions on the topics of acoustic guitar design and amplification.

FRANK FORD

Frank Ford has been a full-time professional luthier since he and his partner, Richard Johnston, founded Gryphon Stringed Instruments in 1969. Ford has written repair articles for a number of publications, and he currently serves on the board of directors of the Association of Stringed Instrument Artisans (ASIA). He is a regular guest instructor at the Roberto-Venn School of Luthiery in Phoenix, Arizona, and at the American School of Lutherie in Healdsburg, California. He created and maintains frets.com, the largest acoustic instrument maintenance and repair reference site on the Internet.

TEJA GERKEN

Teja Gerken is a San Francisco Bay Area fingerstyle guitarist. Before he became *Acoustic Guitar* magazine's gear editor, he managed a music store, apprenticed with a guitar maker in Paracho, Mexico, and worked as a freelance translator and desktop publisher. When he is not busy reviewing gear, visiting guitar factories, or attending trade shows, Gerken hosts a fingerstyle concert series at an Emeryville, California, venue called Strings, where he has shared the stage with many of today's top pickers. His Web site, www.tejagerken.com, features articles on a variety of guitar-related subjects as well as samples of his debut CD *On My Way* (LifeRhythm Music).

STEVE JAMES

Steve James is a touring performer and recording artist based in Austin, Texas. His original music and arrangements for guitar, slide guitar, mandolin, and guitar-banjo can be heard on his own albums and those of numerous other singers and players, including the Bad Livers, Gary Primich, James McMurtry, Angela Strehli, Ana Egge, and Jesse Thomas. James' albums include *Two Track Mind, American Primitive,* and *Art and Grit.* He tours throughout the U.S. and Canada, Europe, South America, and Australia. For more information, visit his Web site at www.stevejames.com.

RICHARD JOHNSTON

Richard Johnston is a luthier, stringed-instrument repairman, and co-owner of Gryphon Stringed Instruments in Palo Alto, California. He is also coauthor, with Jim Washburn, of the book *Martin Guitars: An Illustrated Celebration of America's Premier Guitarmaker* (Rodale Press). Johnston has been writing for *Acoustic Guitar* magazine since its inception in 1990 and has been a contributing editor since 1995. He has written definitive, historical articles on a wide variety of guitars, including vintage flattops, archtops, dreadnoughts, 12-frets, and the Gibson J-200.

MARSHALL NEWMAN

Marshall Newman, a native Californian, first discovered guitars at age 12, when his father purchased an old acoustic at the local gas station. He soon taught himself to play and adopted the instrument, which has remained a faithful friend for nearly 40 years. As proprietor of Newman Communications, Newman now writes marketing and public relations material for several of California's best-known wineries. He recently began trying to master the art of flatpicking, so far without success.

KRISTINA OLSEN

Kristina Olsen is one of the most entertaining and compelling performers on the international folk circuit today. A fine instrumentalist (acoustic guitar, steel-body slide guitar, saxophone, concertina, and piano) as well as a powerful songwriter with a big, bluesy voice, Olsen has audiences around the world coming back for more. She's on the road about ten months per year and has released nine recordings. Her latest is *The Truth of a Woman* (Take a Break).

JACK PEARSON

Jack Pearson is one of those unusual musicians who appeals to kids and grown-ups alike. In 1965 he discovered the guitar at a campfire, and from there it was banjo, mandolin, fiddle, jaw harp, spoons, and songs on a journey that continues to this day. Each year, Pearson performs at K–6 schools, churches, and conference centers around the country. His recordings have won the Parents' Choice Gold and Storytelling World Honor awards, and his songs are featured on family-oriented radio stations around the United States.

SIMONE SOLONDZ

Simone Solondz took her first guitar lesson when she was a junior at the University of Pennsylvania in Philadelphia. She began working at *Acoustic Guitar* magazine in 1991 and has been managing editor since 1996. Solondz first became interested in the inner workings of the acoustic guitar at an Association of Stringed Instrument Artisans symposium in 1993, and she soon began writing articles on the topic geared toward players with limited backgrounds in design and woodworking. She began studying mandolin in 1993 and has since built her own mandolin under the tutelage of Michael Hornick.

BOB TAYLOR

Bob Taylor and his partner Kurt Listug began their guitar-making enterprise (first known as the American Dream and later as Taylor Guitars) in Lemon Grove, California, in 1973. From the start, they ignored preconceived notions of guitar design in favor of their own ideas and techniques. Taylor has been a pioneer in the use of CAD/CAM technology in building guitars and also led the charge in making bolt-on necks an accepted industry standard. He has always been more than willing to share his knowledge with other luthiers at various educational forums, including ASIA symposiums and the Acoustic Guitar Festival.

RICK TURNER

Rick Turner has been designing, building, and repairing acoustic and electric guitars for 35 years. He cofounded the Alembic Corp. in the '70s, worked for the Gibson Guitar Corp., and later started his own cutting-edge company, Turner Guitars. He also designed magnetic pickups and cofounded Highlander Musical Audio Products. Turner is currently president of the Renaissance Guitar Corp. and is working on an acoustic guitar for Henry Kaiser that is slated to travel to the South Pole. He is also a regular contributor to *Acoustic Guitar* magazine and has been a contributing editor since 1991.

An Acoustic Guitar Primer

Teja Gerken

Even if you've been playing your guitar for decades, you may not be entirely clear about what type of acoustic guitar you've got. The terminology people use can be confusing. Is it a flattop? A dreadnought? A classical guitar? Was it designed for jazz music? Bluegrass? Rock 'n' roll? Does it make a difference? Well, these days players at all levels are crossing the boundaries between styles of music and styles of guitar. Classical guitars are wielded by country players, and Hawaiian guitars are showing up in the hands of rock stars. The bottom line is, if you're happy with your instrument, it doesn't really matter what the guitar was originally intended for.

Different kinds of guitars do, however, have different requirements for maintenance and setup. Let's look at the basic types of acoustic guitars and the special features they offer.

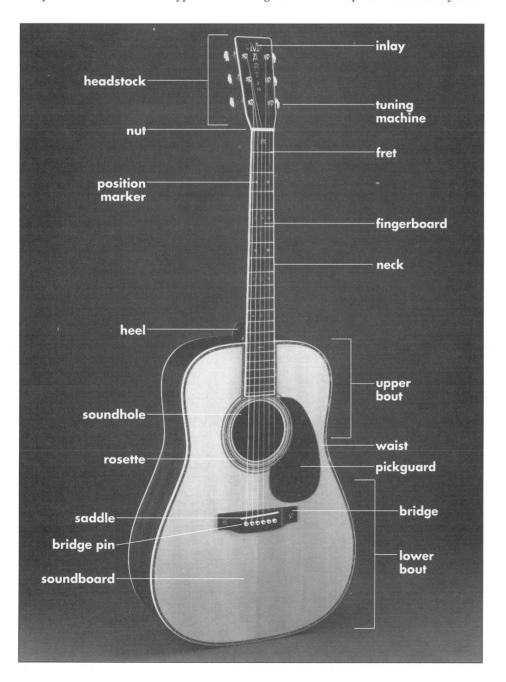

FLATTOP

Flattop steel-string guitars are the most popular acoustic guitars in America. They're used in many musical genres, including folk, pop, rock, bluegrass, and fingerstyle instrumental. They come in a wide variety of sizes—everything from the tiny parlor guitar to the gigantic jumbo—with the Martin-style dreadnought being the most common. These instruments were designed for steel strings. Most of them are descendents of American guitars built shortly after the turn of the century by large manufacturers such as C.F. Martin and Co. and Gibson. Nowadays, the majority of flattops are built in factories, but many individual luthiers build them as well. Prices range from around $200 to several thousand, with quality levels to match.

The tops are typically built of spruce, but some makers also use cedar, mahogany, or koa. A plastic pickguard is usually glued to the top near the soundhole to protect the wood from pick scratches. Rosewood and mahogany are commonly used for the backs and sides, but maple, koa, and a variety of other woods are also quite popular. The vast majority of necks are built of mahogany and feature rosewood or ebony fingerboards. The tops of these guitars are generally braced with an X pattern originally made popular by Martin, and the braces themselves are commonly "scalloped," which means that wood is scooped out of the middle of the brace, allowing it to vibrate more freely.

Other common features are the pin bridge designed for ball-end steel strings; the solid headstock with individual, enclosed tuning machines (although many vintage and vintage-inspired flattops feature a classical-style slotted headstock); and the adjustable truss rod embedded in the neck, which allows you to tweak the bow of the neck depending on such factors as humidity and string gauge. Traditionally, the neck is joined to the body with a dovetail joint, but many modern guitars feature bolt-on or mortise-and-tenon designs. Typical neck designs feature 14 or 12 frets clear of the body, and scale lengths (the distance from the nut to the bridge) range from 24¾ to 25½ inches. Most flattop steel-strings have a slightly curved fingerboard and inlaid position markers at the third, fifth, seventh, ninth, 12th, 15th, and 17th frets.

FLATTOP BODY SIZES (BASED ON C.F. MARTIN MODEL DESIGNATIONS)

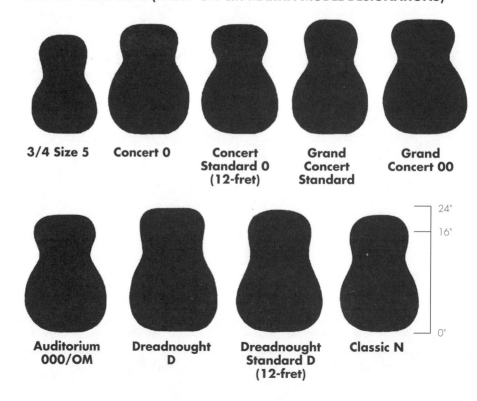

3/4 Size 5   **Concert 0**   **Concert Standard 0 (12-fret)**   **Grand Concert Standard**   **Grand Concert 00**

Auditorium 000/OM   **Dreadnought D**   **Dreadnought Standard D (12-fret)**   **Classic N**

CLASSICAL

Classical guitars are designed for nylon strings (plain on the top three strings and wound on the bottom three) and therefore feature much lighter construction than their steel-string cousins. They're often called nylon-strings; some people also refer to them as gut-strings, a reflection of the material used before the adoption of nylon in the mid-20th century. They are generally smaller in size and have wider necks and flat finger-boards to facilitate classical technique. The headstocks are slotted, and the bridges are designed to have nylon strings tied onto them. They tend to lack pickguards and fingerboard inlays, and they usually feature elaborate mosaic-style rosettes around their soundholes. Most builders brace the top in a fan pattern that originated in Spain in the mid-19th century. Rosewood is by far the most popular wood for the back and sides, although some luthiers also use mahogany or maple, among other choices. About half of the classical soundboards out there are made of spruce and the other half of cedar, and a few luthiers are experimenting with alternatives such as redwood. Although classical guitars aren't as popular in the U.S. as steel-strings, globally they are the most common. Factory-made classical guitars are produced around the world, but serious players usually choose handmade instruments.

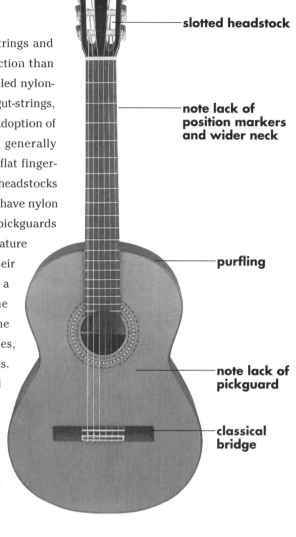

slotted headstock

note lack of position markers and wider neck

purfling

note lack of pickguard

classical bridge

FLAMENCO

The flamenco guitar is similar to the classical guitar and uses the same nylon strings, but it differs in a few important areas. The flamenco guitar is traditionally constructed very lightly with cypress back and sides (although the rosewood *flamenca negra* is becoming increasingly popular) and has a bright, percussive sound. The original flamenco design also features a solid headstock with violin-style friction pegs (but most contemporary flamenco guitars use standard classical tuning machines), and the bodies of many of these instruments are more shallow than those of typical classical guitars. A clear plastic *golpeador* or tap plate protects the top from the aggressive right-hand techniques employed by flamenco players. The action on this type of guitar is generally very low, making it easy to play and likely to buzz slightly (a desired effect in flamenco music). The majority of flamenco guitars are built in small shops, but a few entry-level models are available from larger manufacturers.

friction peg

ARCHTOP

The archtop guitar was born during the early days of jazz and borrows many of its design traits from violins and mandolins. It was initially developed for volume; it had to compete in large bands and orchestras before the advent of electronic amplification. The archtop guitar has a carved, arched top (on many inexpensive archtops, the arch is actually pressed into the top with the help of steam). These guitars project their sound very well and have a fast attack with less sustain than most flattops. While some early models used glued-on pin bridges, the bridges of most modern archtops are held in place by string pressure, and a *trapeze tailpiece* (similar to a mandolin tailpiece) anchors the strings to the butt of the instrument. Violin-style f-holes have become the most popular soundhole for archtops, although round soundholes have been used since the instrument's earliest days, and some modern luthiers are now experimenting with alternative soundhole placements. The tops of these guitars are virtually always made of spruce, and maple and mahogany are the most popular choices for backs and sides. While archtop soundboards are traditionally braced with two lateral tone bars, some newer designs feature X-bracing similar to those found in flattops.

A true acoustic archtop will either have no pickup or a *floating pickup* mounted at the end of the fingerboard. Archtops with pickups mounted into their tops are generally intended for electric use and have a compromised acoustic sound. With the exception of some entry-level models and vintage examples, the acoustic archtop market is dominated by individual luthiers, and archtop guitars are among the most expensive guitars currently made.

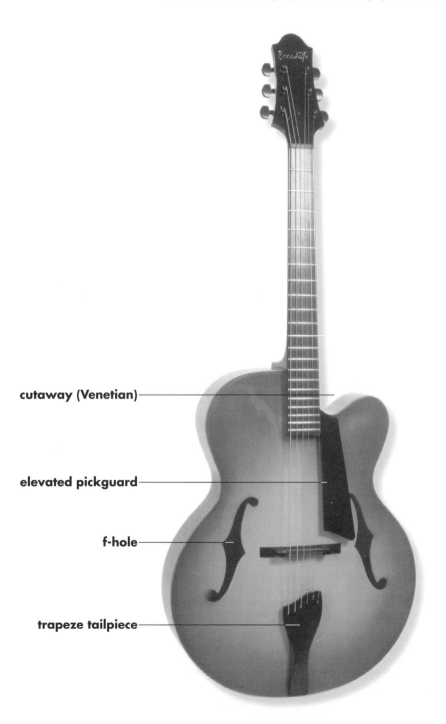

cutaway (Venetian)

elevated pickguard

f-hole

trapeze tailpiece

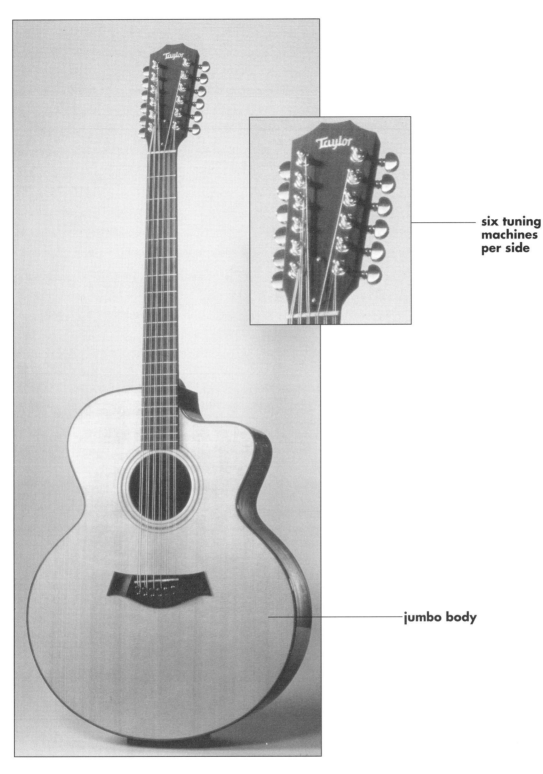

six tuning
machines
per side

jumbo body

12-STRING

The 12-string guitar features (you guessed it) 12 strings strung in courses of two, tuned
E E A A D D G G B B E E, where the strings of the four bottom pairs are an octave apart
and the strings of the top two pairs sound in unison. (Some instruments are designed to
be tuned a whole step or more lower.) The instrument is more difficult to play than a six-
string but produces a big, complex sound (think Leo Kottke or Leadbelly). The typical
12-string features a flattop design that's strong enough to withstand the additional string
tension. Some 12-strings—such as those made by Guild and Rickenbacker—feature double truss rods to keep the neck from bowing forward. For ultimate volume and bass
response, many players prefer a jumbo 12-string design. It's not difficult to find a 12-
string; most large manufacturers offer 12-string models.

ACOUSTIC-ELECTRIC

Almost every type of acoustic guitar is now available as an acoustic-electric. Some acoustic-electrics simply feature an added pickup (usually a piezo pickup under the saddle) on an existing acoustic guitar, while others are built from the ground up with electronics in mind. In many cases, acoustic-electrics have smaller, shallower bodies and stiffer tops that don't vibrate as much. These traits can compromise acoustic sound, but they help battle feedback at high volumes. Some instruments dubbed "acoustic-electric" are actually solid-bodies with no acoustic sound to speak of. Their piezo pickups allow the player to produce an approximation of the acoustic sound on stage with practically no feedback problems. Internal preamps and on-board controls are often a selling point of the acoustic-electric, and some new systems even include an internal microphone, which, blended with the pickup, can produce a more natural acoustic sound on stage.

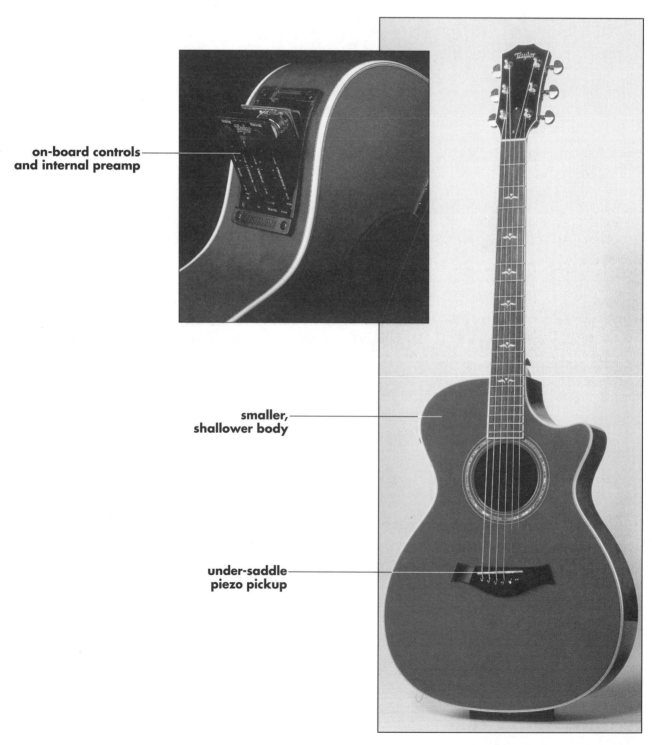

on-board controls and internal preamp

smaller, shallower body

under-saddle piezo pickup

RESONATOR

Like archtops, resonator guitars were designed to be loud before electronic amplification was available. There's actually a metal resonator inside the body that's producing the sound. Spun out of thin aluminum, the resonator's cone acts like a loudspeaker, resulting in a very loud and distinctive sound. On single-cone instruments, distinctions are made between *spider* and *biscuit* resonators, and the tricone models use three small resonators. The guitar body can be made of wood or metal. Resonator guitars can be played like flattops or lap-style with a slide. For the best sound, these guitars are usually strung with heavy steel strings. The vast majority of resonator guitars are made by the Dobro and National Reso-Phonic companies, with a few small shops and inexpensive imports competing for market share.

heavy strings

metal body

resonator(s) inside

hand rest

protective plate

engraving

tailpiece

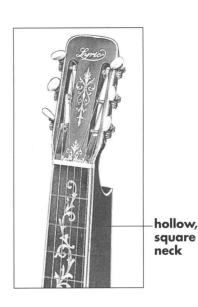

HAWAIIAN

Hawaiian guitars are designed to be played lap-style with a steel bar for a slide. These instruments can range from what are basically standard steel-string flattops set up with very high action, to special hollow-neck guitars—such as vintage Weissenborns and Knutsens—which can only be played lap-style and often feature painted-on frets. They are strung with heavy strings, usually tuned to an open chord. Vintage originals are becoming increasingly rare and expensive, and there are several independent luthiers and small shops offering contemporary versions.

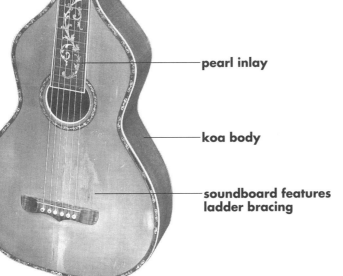

pearl inlay

koa body

soundboard features ladder bracing

hollow, square neck

Inside Your Guitar

Rick Turner

Inner space: an unusual perspective on the work of Israeli guitar maker Boaz Elkayam.

When you pick up your acoustic guitar, strum a chord, and let that sweet sound wash over you, you are hearing the result of a complex and delicate interaction of the myriad parts of your instrument. What do the different elements of your guitar contribute to its sound? How can a luthier shape its tonal character? What is the most crucial element in a great instrument—the design, the materials, or the craftsmanship? Guitar makers around the globe have wrestled with these questions for centuries, but today's luthiers probably know more about the answers than anyone has before.

Acoustic guitars are amazingly subtle and versatile instruments that are constantly undergoing design changes and redefinition by luthiers and musicians worldwide. What we think of as the classical guitar is barely 150 years old, the archtop guitar is just 100 years old, and the now-omnipresent dreadnought first appeared less than 70 years ago. Contemporary luthiers are pushing the envelope with new construction details and shapes and paying a lot of attention to scientific input into the physics of how a guitar produces sound. Materials, too, are changing: the use of synthetics in guitars such as Maccaferris and Ovations has come in our generation. Future musicians may recognize our era as the time when the acoustic guitar came of age.

The body of knowledge from which guitar makers draw has increased tremendously in the lutherie renaissance of the last 30 years. Books, videos, catalogs, kits, and networking organizations freely share what used to be known only in a few masters' workshops. Along with open lines of communication among luthiers, manufacturers, and players, a deeper understanding of how guitars work and what makes some better than others has emerged. While there will always be differences of opinion regarding particular designs, woods, and approaches to the instrument, we have more control over getting a desired result than ever. In this chapter we'll look at some of the principles that guide the sound and feel of today's guitars.

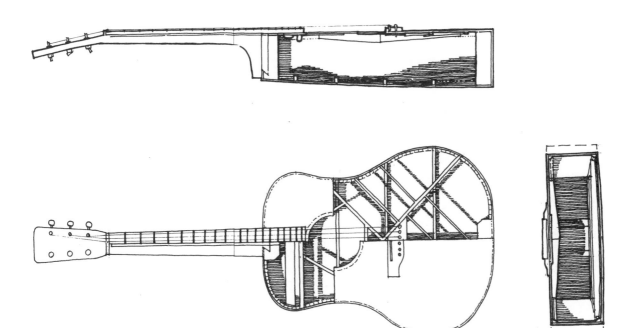

FROM STRING ENERGY TO SOUND

One of the terms often used to refer to the transformation of string energy into acoustic energy is *amplification,* a word that leads to a fundamental misunderstanding of how acoustic guitars produce sound. Implicit in the concept of amplification, as used in electrical engineering, is the presence of an external power source that is being modulated by the original signal in order to raise the power level. But an acoustic guitar acts according to a mechanical, not an electrical, model. You might think of an acoustic guitar as being like a playground seesaw: by moving the fulcrum point, you can balance the weights and leg-muscle forces of two people of vastly different sizes. Using that analogy, the guitar bridge saddle is the balancing point between string motion and top motion.

Guitar strings are simply small, round lengths of wire that cut through the air rather than setting up audible acoustical waves. To hear how little output a string has, play a heavy electric guitar unplugged—there's not much there. An acoustic guitar body takes the acoustically inefficient motion of the strings and transforms it into the vibration of a much larger plate—the top—which is better suited to moving a mass of air and thus producing sound. So in a purely acoustic guitar, no outside energy is added to that of the string vibration; there is only a change in the medium carrying the vibration. No real amplification occurs. You cannot get more energy out of an acoustic guitar than what your hands put into it.

The interface between the string and the rest of the guitar is the bridge, which transfers the string motion into the top through a combination of rocking and shaking. The bridge must be large enough to transmit the vibration to the whole top, yet light enough that its mass doesn't slow down the top's movement. In fact, one of the tricks I use when a client complains of too little treble on a guitar is to lighten the bridge as much as possible while still retaining reasonable strength and stiffness. One way to think of the bridge is as the most important and complex brace on the top.

FROM THE TOP

The goal of the luthier is to make an instrument that most efficiently transforms string energy into aesthetically pleasing acoustic radiation. The primary means for achieving this goal is in the design of the soundboard. This is why guitar makers pay so much

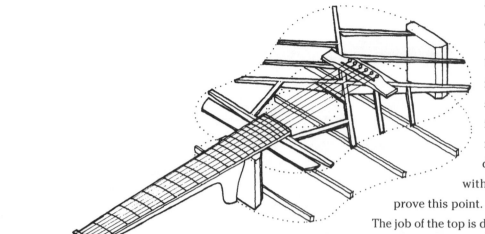

The drawing shows how the bridge acts as a brace in the context of a typical dreadnought's bracing system.

attention to top wood and bracing. Of course, all the parts of a guitar have to work in concert with the top. The back, sides, neck, fingerboard, and frets add their signatures to the sound, but the top remains supreme in transforming string motion into air motion. The Spanish luthier Antonio de Torres even made a classical guitar with back and sides of papier-mâché to prove this point.

The job of the top is daunting: it must be lightweight enough to respond quickly, yet it must support the torque, strain, and pressure of 120 to nearly 190 pounds of constant string pull. The top must radiate energy efficiently, yet vibration must be controlled so that the top works as much as possible as a single unit. The top is also the primary acoustic equalizer for the strings; it filters out some notes and harmonics while enhancing others. It is the "voicing" or "tuning" of the top that makes or breaks a luthier's reputation.

Through the filter of time, luthiers and musicians have come to nearly universal agreement that straight-grained, quartersawn spruce, cedar, and redwood are the first three choices for top wood, followed by mahogany and koa. Scientific data shows that these woods all have high stiffness-to-weight ratios, moderate density, and relatively low damping of vibration; and they all exhibit good sound transmission velocity. These factors add up to minimal loss of energy and maximum transformation of string energy into acoustic power.

A great deal of controversy surrounds which wood subspecies are best, but this is like arguing over favorite recipes. Each luthier develops a wood characteristics recipe for what becomes his or her signature sound. None of the differences among Sitka, Engelmann, Adirondack, and European spruce change the basics of how the guitars function. In fact, some of the best luthiers seem to be able to work just about any wood for its maximum tone. Take a look at the knotty-pine–topped archtop in Bob Benedetto's book *Making an Archtop Guitar,* for instance. Benedetto made that guitar to prove the point that a good maker can build a decent guitar out of practically anything.

Through trial and error, luthiers have developed techniques for bracing guitar tops that enhance strength while minimizing weight. In many ways, this developing technology parallels what has happened in architecture and structural engineering over the past 1,000 years. It's all about getting higher performance out of less material by learning about how the elements work together to resist stresses and, in the case of instruments, produce sound.

Bracing also controls how the top vibrates, and this fact leads to a lot of voodoo: tone bars, scalloped versus nonscalloped braces, flying top supports, tapered braces, square braces, laminated braces, etc. Bracing is a real balancing act; too much and the guitar won't "speak," too little and the guitar will collapse. If the edges are too stiff, the guitar will not develop its bass potential; but if they're too floppy, the guitar will just boom. And these are just the easy-to-identify features.

In the last 20 years there has been a virtual explosion of interest in a more scientific approach to bracing guitars, with Dr. Michael Kasha and Greg Smallman leading the way, mostly in the classical guitar field (an ironic situation, because classical guitarists tend to be conservative and resistant to changes in instrument design). Laser holography photos reveal that guitar tops tend to break up at various frequencies; different sections of the top actually vibrate in and out of phase, leading to acoustic cancellation (see photos on page 20). The goal of many modern luthiers is to use the bracing to control the way vibrations travel through and emanate from the top, and this has led to a variety of experiments in bracing patterns and top thickness graduation.

The earliest guitars had ladder bracing, lateral stiffeners derived from earlier instruments like the lute and its ancestor, the Arabic oud. Ladder bracing probably evolved from observation of the distortion pattern of unbraced instrument tops. Early luthiers supported areas that sank down and bubbled up as string tension torqued and stressed the top. There's nothing like a broken instrument to inspire new designs.

Ladder bracing is still used almost exclusively on backs of acoustic guitars, where stresses are not as concentrated as on the top. Even though ladder bracing on the top has been passed over by most modern luthiers, there are still some—such as Marc Silber—who advocate this "archaic" system. Perhaps ladder bracing has gotten an undeserved bad rap from its usage on so many thousands of cheap and generally overbuilt guitars. It is clear that if you want a 12-string that sounds like Leadbelly's famous Stella, or you want the sound of an early 19th-century guitar, ladder bracing is the way to go.

In the late 18th and early 19th centuries, European luthiers, primarily in Spain and France, started experimenting successfully with fan bracing. (Torres is often incorrectly credited with inventing this method of strengthening guitar tops.) With the change from ladder to fan, luthiers started to realize that at least some of the braces could be considered "tone bars": these braces were not just holding the guitar together, but also developing particular tonal qualities by controlling the vibration in the top.

Christian Frederick Martin, whose earliest guitars were ladder braced, developed and perfected the X-bracing system in the 1850s. While it is debatable whether Martin was the first to X-brace a guitar top, there is no doubt that this was one of the most important changes of the past 150 years in acoustic guitar design. However, Martin perfected the X for gut strings; it was not until the early 1920s that the Martin company regularly put steel strings on its guitars. Whatever the original intent of the X, it would prove to be the most popular bracing pattern of all time for the increased tension of steel strings.

Michael Kasha, a professor of molecular biology and a classical guitar aficionado, has applied his experience in scientific investigation to the matter of matching different string frequencies to the acoustic guitar top. Working closely with late classical guitar maker Richard Schneider and steel-string builder Steve Klein, Kasha developed a guitar bracing

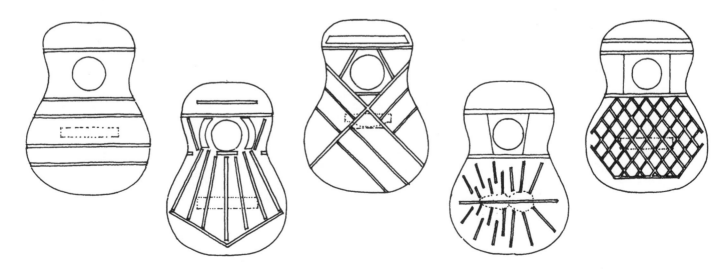

The diagrams (left to right) depict the following top bracing designs: ladder, classical fan, X, Kasha, and Smallman.

pattern that works like the crossover in a speaker system, attempting to maximize the coupling efficiency at different frequencies by using longer braces on the bass side and shorter ones on the treble side, arrayed in a radial pattern.

Down in Australia, Greg Smallman has taken the "guitar as speaker cone" approach to new technological heights, and his instruments are championed by classical virtuoso John Williams for their responsiveness, particularly in the upper harmonics. Smallman braces the top with a lattice of spruce and carbon fiber (graphite), making the center of the top very stiff yet extremely lightweight. The edges of the top are thinned out and reinforced by individually laid-up carbon fibers, with the goal of making the top plate move as a unit, minimizing the usual in-and-out-of-phase vibrations that cancel upper partials.

The archtop guitar is a somewhat different animal when it comes to how the top works. Developed by Orville Gibson and perfected by Lloyd Loar and generations of other Gibson designers, John D'Angelico, the Strombergs, Epiphone, and now a new generation of builders, the archtop is based on the violin model, in which the arching of the top itself creates a great deal of structural strength. Archtop guitars are generally fitted with tailpieces, eliminating torque from the stresses on the top. There is less "breakup" of the top at mid and high frequencies, leading to great clarity in the best examples. While archtops often don't sound as loud to the player as do similar-sized flattops, their projection and cutting power can be awesome; think of Freddie Green playing acoustically in the Count Basie Orchestra. Archtops tend to focus on a more limited range of frequencies than do flattops, which increases the acoustic power in that chosen range.

Stefan Sobell, an English luthier, has combined some of the strength and tonal clarity of the archtop with a more flattop type of design. His guitar tops are bent into a mild cylindrical arch, with X-braces further supporting the tension of the strings. His guitars have great definition and very wide dynamic range, like good archtops, but they also have more of the bass response you would expect from a flattop.

 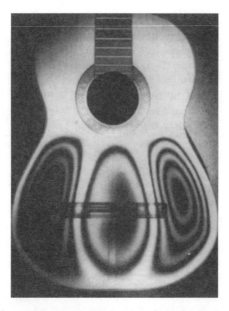 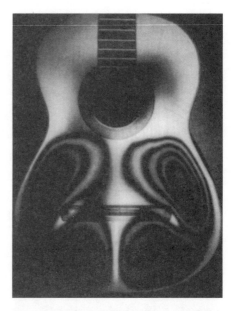

Laser holography photos show how vibrations in a guitar's top break up at characteristic frequencies into modal patterns, with some parts of the top moving out of phase with other parts. These photos taken in 1969 by Karl Stetson and Nils-Erik Molin show the same guitar top responding to 287 Hz, 460 Hz (a little higher than a middle A), and 645 Hz.

There are many other patterns and methods used to brace tops, but the foregoing are the highlights of contemporary guitars. Most individual guitar makers modify the bracing patterns and dimensions as they go along, trying to get the most out of each combination of top wood and brace wood. For stiffer top wood, bracing can be lighter than normal; for more flexible wood, heavier bracing is necessary. Some manufacturers, such as the Santa Cruz Guitar Co., grade their wood so the floppier tops go on smaller guitars, enhancing bass, while the stiffer wood goes on jumbos and dreadnoughts, helping to bring out the trebles. Bracing is matched to both the wood characteristics and the size of the guitar.

RESONANCE

Each structure, tensed string, and enclosed air space has a resonant frequency, and the more specific the resonant frequency, the more efficiently it can oscillate with minimal energy input. Resonators are like Steve Martin with his happy shoes on—they just *have* to dance. Chances are good you're wearing a resonator on your wrist; the quartz crystal that regulates the speed of your watch is an efficient resonator whose vibrational frequency is electronically stimulated and then divided to give you seconds, minutes, and hours.

Resonance is not necessarily a measure of quality, as in, "This guitar is really resonant!" Rather, it is a factor that can be exploited in making strings speak through the medium of the guitar. Resonances are what add character to sound, although they must be controlled so that they don't completely take over.

An acoustic guitar is a whole collection of resonators. The strings are tunable resonators of very high efficiency; plucking them gets them moving at a discrete frequency determined by their weight, length, and tension. The guitar top has a primary resonant frequency along with many resonances of lesser strength; so does the back. The neck, too, has resonances both in flexure and in twisting motion. Each piece of wood in the guitar has its own resonance, although the individual resonances are greatly modified when the pieces are glued together. There is also a factor of antiresonance, the point at which frequencies are diminished through cancellation. With some instruments, a resonance in one part can actually suck the vibration out of the strings, leading to dead notes. In these cases, string energy is being lost as heat in the structure of the guitar.

The air-cavity resonance of an acoustic guitar is also important in establishing acoustic output. The box is a resonator that reinforces the bass response of the instrument by coupling a tuned air chamber to the outside air. Manipulating the internal air volume of a guitar is one way luthiers can increase or decrease its low-end response. A perfect example is the Nick Lucas style of Gibson guitar; it has a relatively deep body for its outline size. Compare the tone of a typical Nick Lucas with its shallower near equivalent, the 00-sized Martin: the Lucas has more lows.

The tone of an acoustic guitar is the sum of all its resonances and antiresonances. Each element used in its construction adds or subtracts from the basic "pure" tone of the strings, which are the primary tone generators. The challenge of lutherie is to combine all these vibrating parts into a pleasing whole that responds evenly while retaining character.

THE NECK FACTOR

The materials and construction techniques used to make necks and fingerboards contribute to the tone, attack, and sustain of guitars and basses. Oddly, there has probably been more attention paid to these factors in the electric instrument field than with acoustics, because there is little "acousticity" to mask these effects in electric instruments.

Guitar necks must be stiff enough to resist string pull, and the neck should also resist being put into motion by the strings, which results in lost energy. More and more luthiers are using new materials to modify the performance of traditional wood necks. Dana Bourgeois, for instance, uses two rigid steel bars in addition to an adjustable truss rod in his mahogany necks, gaining both stiffness and mass. Many other luthiers, myself included, are burying space-age graphite composites in wood necks to gain the benefits of added stiffness without the added weight of steel.

The fingerboard adds a tonal signature as well. Ebony, the most traditional of fingerboard woods, is dense, stiff, smooth, and has a fairly low Q or resonance factor. It is known for contributing sustain and tonal smoothness a bit on the "dark" side. Although no longer available, Brazilian rosewood is another traditional choice; it can offer a bit more snap than ebony. Woods like Indian rosewood and maple have their own tonal characteristics, based on how they selectively absorb or reflect the energy transmitted by the frets.

Even a seemingly insignificant factor such as fret size and hardness makes a difference. The matter of fret wire size has long been recognized in the electric guitar world, and I've noticed that classical guitarists, finding that sustain and attack are improved by having the strings terminate at a higher mass, are now favoring larger and larger fret wire.

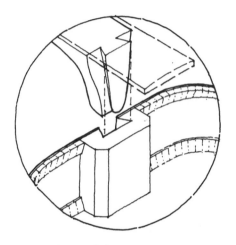

A 3-D view of the traditional dovetail neck-to-body joint, with a detailed close-up below. Note how the neck drops into its slot from above the guitar's top.

Another trend in fingerboard design, at least in steel-string guitars, is a curved fingerboard with a tighter radius. Typically on classical guitars, the fingerboard is dead flat, with a slight twisting drop-off toward the bass side over the body. However, on steel-string guitars it is common to make the fingerboard curved as a section of either a cylinder or cone. The radius of the arc is usually in the range of 12–17 inches, though on some electric guitars, the radius may be as small as nine inches.

The tighter radiuses are thought to be more comfortable for closed and barred chording, while the flatter fingerboards allow lower action for players who bend notes a lot in the higher positions. It is fairly common these days to find electric guitars with compound radius fingerboards: nine or ten inches at the first fret and 15–17 inches at the 20th fret. For some players, this is the best of both worlds.

THE NECK-TO-BODY CONNECTION

Twenty years ago, no guitarist would have paid attention to a guitar with anything but a traditionally dovetailed neck joint. The theory was that a good, tightly glued neck joint did the best job of transferring energy to the body. Tell that to anyone who plays a Taylor, Bourgeois, Noble, or Collings. They all have bolt-on necks, and no one is complaining about loss of tone. Clearly, if a neck joint is loose or vibrates, energy is lost, but as long as the neck is secure, it doesn't matter how it is attached.

In fact, there is very little if any transfer of useful string energy through the neck joint into the body. Try holding a tuning fork to a guitar's side next to the neck to see how much vibration is transferred to the top and out as sound: not much! If anything, the neck should not absorb string vibration but reflect that energy back into the top, which is designed for transforming energy into acoustic waves.

MATERIAL WORLD

Over several hundred years, luthiers have settled on a relatively small collection of materials with which to build guitars. Woods from both the hardwood and softwood categories are used extensively. It is interesting to scientifically evaluate the measurable qualities of the various woods chosen and see how appropriate the traditional choices were. Every type of wood—in fact, each piece of wood—is made up of a recipe that includes density, resonance, damping, strength, dimensional stability, stiffness, toughness, and appearance. Passed down with traditional wood preferences is a kind of inescapable logic that helps define just what a guitar is. Those luthiers who choose to deviate far from the tradition risk making guitars so different that they alienate, rather than entice, musicians.

For top woods and bracing, various subspecies of spruce are the most accepted, and many luthiers are now using cedar and old-growth sequoia redwood. All of these woods have excellent stiffness-to-weight ratios, are moderately resonant, and are relatively stable when properly cured and cut. These woods are invariably cut "on the quarter" with minimal grain run-out. This means that the cut maximizes the continuous length of the wood fibers, increasing strength and stiffness relative to weight.

Neck woods need to be stiffer, stronger, and more dense to withstand string tension and handling; stability is also very important, as even moderate wood movement can lead to very noticeable changes in the guitar's action. Spanish cedar, Honduras mahogany, and maple are the common choices here, with many individual luthiers also using the rosewoods, walnut, and various other stable woods. As far as wood figure goes, straight grain is best for a neck; highly figured woods are inherently less stable. One possible exception to this is bird's-eye maple, which seems to retain the stiffness and stability of plain maple.

Fingerboard wood choice, too, has narrowed to include little more than ebony and the various rosewoods, chosen primarily for resistance to wear. Electric guitarists may also choose maple, but there has been very little use of other species by acoustic-guitar makers, with the exception of Ovation's use of acrylic-impregnated walnut.

As some of the traditionally used woods virtually disappear (Brazilian rosewood is now on an international embargo list, ebonies are increasingly hard to obtain, etc.), luthiers are looking to woods that can be farmed on plantations or otherwise responsibly harvested, and they are also experimenting with new composite materials that mimic the qualities of wood and even go beyond wood in certain respects. For my own guitars, I am trying out pakka wood, a dyed birch veneer/phenolic laminate that looks great and shows promise as a fingerboard material. I'm also looking into a wood stabilization process similar to the one Ovation uses, whereby woods are vacuum-impregnated with a methacrylic resin that lines the walls of the wood cells, making the wood denser, tougher, and extremely resistant to humidity changes. Graphite epoxy composites are being used very effectively by many luthiers as a means of either replacing wood, as in RainSong guitars, or enhancing the performance of wood. Properly used, graphite can add tremendous stiffness while reducing weight.

Even the materials used for string nuts and bridge saddles can have a major effect on tone, because they affect how the strings interact with the rest of the guitar. String nuts made in the traditional manner guide the strings and set the action of the open strings. If

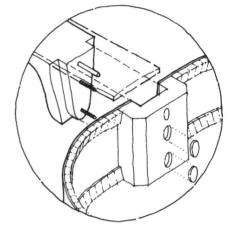

The same perspectives of the bolt-on neck used by luthier Bill Collings. The neck attaches to the body with a mortise joint, which allows the bolts to drop directly into the holes in the neckblock.

made of too soft a material, the string nut can damp string vibrations, so I actually prefer to use a zero fret—an extra fret at the end of the fingerboard where the nut is ordinarily situated—that lets the nut act merely as a string guide. The idea is to use a material that makes open notes sound the same as fretted notes. What could do that job better than fret wire? Most players, however, have no problem with the tone provided by a regular bone nut, and the zero fret is relatively rare.

The bridge saddle is the ultimate "witness point" at the interface between the strings and the top. Poor materials used here damp the string and prevent the full range of harmonic information from reaching the guitar top. Modern amplified acoustic guitars generally use under-saddle pickups to translate string motion into an electrical signal, and in this application, the proper saddle material and correct fitting can make the difference between a great-sounding guitar and a dud. Elephant ivory has been the top choice for saddles for many years, but it is now an ethically dubious preference. Bleached cow bone is the common substitute these days, with fossil ivories—generally mastodon or walrus—being the high-end choice. Some artificial materials are now coming into common use; they offer the promise of greater consistency than what is usually found in the natural products.

IN YOUR HANDS

As a musician, you can get more out of your guitar by better understanding how it works, and by accepting and working with the limitations inherent in its design and construction. The constant struggle for guitar makers is to build lightly enough to make a responsive instrument, yet robustly enough so the instrument can hold up to string tension and at least moderate abuse. You should not expect a fine guitar to be a maintenance-free product; if you want great tone, you're going to have to take care of a delicate structure whose dimensions will vary along with changes in season, humidity, and temperature. Also, wood will slowly change shape under the constant strain of string tension. You would, too, if you had to carry more than 150 pounds on your belly for the rest of your life!

Bob Taylor of Taylor Guitars has extensively researched the dimensional changes that occur in acoustic guitars and how these changes affect playability and structural integrity. These types of changes are accepted in the violin world, where playing instruments that are 100 to 300 years old is fairly common. Guitarists, on the other hand, seem to expect their instruments to go through about as many changes as a pet rock. Guitars are a bit like fine automobiles: they get dinged, things wear out and need replacement, regular tune-ups are a good idea, and sometimes they deserve restoration.

Every time I pick up a great acoustic guitar, I am amazed by how it's made and how it works. There are few objects in our lives that so well combine visual aesthetics, musical function, engineering, and long-term usefulness. Look around your house for anything as well designed and expertly made as your acoustic guitar, and say a prayer of thanks.

Fifteen Guitar Myths Debunked

Richard Johnston

Guitar music is an art that people love to get scientific about. Everywhere players get together to talk guitars, whether it's at a festival jam session or on the Internet, someone is theorizing about the mechanical workings of those powerful wooden boxes—particularly about why one guitar sounds better than another. Some of these sound bites get repeated often enough and with such passion that they seem to have the ring of truth, when in fact many of them are little more than the guitar equivalent of urban myths. It's a bit harsh to call these "myths" in the usual sense; "well-intended bits of advice that aren't necessarily based on fact" might be a better term. Many of the widely held beliefs about guitar care are merely overcautious. But some of the myths commonly tossed around can be misleading, especially to someone shopping for a guitar.

1. *A guitar's sound comes out of the soundhole.*

Anyone who has used one of those soundhole plugs to prevent feedback when using a pickup knows that acoustic guitars still make a lot of noise when you tape their mouths shut. The soundboard moves air both inside and outside the guitar when it is activated by string vibration, and sound travels through the spruce as well. Most folks agree that a guitar sounds better when the soundhole(s) are open, however.

2. *Satin finishes are thinner (or more natural) and result in a better sounding guitar than gloss finishes.*

A satin finish isn't much different than gloss in composition, and although the dull sheen makes it look thinner, the film thickness is usually about the same (the exceptions are some inexpensive guitars with almost no finish at all). What most people don't realize is that a satin finish is achieved by adding a chemical to regular lacquer to eliminate the shine when it dries, and that such finishes can be buffed out to look glossy. Satin-finished guitars often develop shiny areas (especially on the neck) where the finish is rubbed as you play. These low-gloss finishes are less expensive for manufacturers because the time-consuming process of rubbing out is eliminated.

3. *Tight-grained spruce tops sound better than those with wide-spaced grain.*

There are too many variables to predict sound based on how many vertical grain lines you can count across a horizontal inch of spruce (the way it's often graded for strength). Old Martins with sound to die for often have spruce with fewer than ten grain lines per

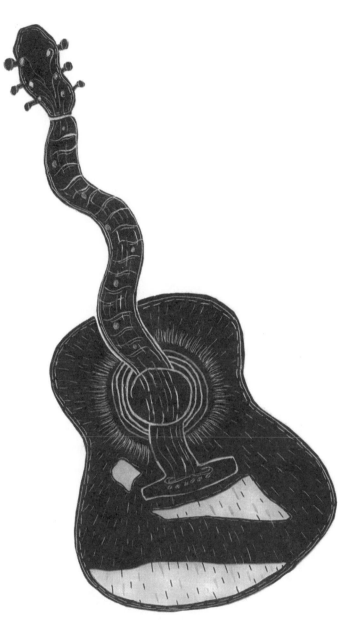

Fears about neck warping can be a little excessive.

inch, but a modern luthier would be shunned for choosing such an "inferior" grade. Stiffness in any wood is determined by more than just the tightness of the grain, and a top that's too stiff can produce an inferior tone. Finally, it's the combination of top and top bracing that counts.

4. Wood used in guitar making should always be quartersawn.

It's certainly true that guitar tops and necks are stronger and more stable if they have vertical grain, but the sides and back are mostly reflective and not under the same structural demands. Lots of highly valued vintage guitars, both classical and steel-string, have what are commonly called "slab cut" backs, and nobody is complaining about the way they sound. And if you like Brazilian rosewood, there is little hope these days of finding quartersawn wood of that species that is wide enough for your dream-boat dreadnought.

5. Cracks in the top ruin the sound.

Actually, lots of people are afraid cracks anywhere in a guitar hurt the sound. Believe it or not, multiple cracks in the soundboard of a guitar will not harm the sound at all if repaired properly, unless they've caused loose braces or other structural weakness. While cracks in the back and sides should also be repaired to prevent them from spreading, they have even less effect on tone or volume. This is not to say that cracks don't hurt the value of a guitar, however.

6. Scalloped-brace guitars always sound better than ones made with straight or merely tapered bracing.

The same logic found in the tight-grained tops myth above can be applied here, and many top-ranked builders do not scallop their top's braces. But in the bad old days, big manufacturers often overbraced their guitars to prevent any chance of a warranty claim, regardless of the string gauge used or how the guitar was mistreated. When scalloped-brace guitars were first made available again 20-plus years ago, they often did sound better than the stiffly braced guitars common to that era.

7. Shaving the braces under the guitar top will make the guitar sound better.

See the previous myth. Shaving top braces is risky business and doesn't yield predictable results, though some production guitars from the '60s and '70s certainly had more bracing than they needed. Finding a lightly braced guitar that already sounds good shouldn't be hard these days.

Cracks in the top don't necessarily spoil the sound.

8. Removing a guitar's pickguard improves the sound.

Some of those big double Everly Brothers pickguards that droop down past the bridge probably do soak up their share of a guitar top's vibration. But most pickguards around the soundhole are lightweight and are fastened to a part of the top that isn't all that critical to guitar tone anyway.

9. *Guitar necks should always be perfectly straight.*

Most guitarists find they get less fret buzz with a slight amount of "relief" (forward curve) in the neck, especially if they play hard on the bass strings in the lower position. Players who have a very precise and even attack, and who use the entire guitar neck, often prefer a neck that is perfectly straight or close to it.

10. *Tying your strap to the peghead (instead of a strap button on the heel) can warp the neck.*

This myth is based on the belief that a guitar neck is in a state of fragile balance against the evil influence of string tension, and any additional tension must be avoided. But steel-string guitar necks are made to withstand over 150 pounds of pull from a set of light strings, so the slight weight from hanging a strap on the neck isn't enough to worry about.

11. *Change the strings on your guitar one at a time.*

Here's that fear of "upsetting the delicate balance" again. There's just no evidence that removing all the strings causes any harm or loss of tone. Removing the strings may allow you to clean the fretboard, making strings last a bit longer since they won't pick up grunge from around the frets. On the other hand, changing strings one at a time allows you to tune up the new string to the rest of the set, avoiding the embarrassment of breaking strings or being hopelessly sharp or flat if you don't have an electronic tuner, tuning fork, or pitch pipe.

12. *Don't fly with your guitar or ship the guitar without loosening the strings, because of the changes in atmospheric pressure.*

Presumably folks are referring to checking the guitar as baggage when they solemnly intone this one. It's the delicate balance issue again, but this time the myth results in sound advice given for the wrong reason. Though lots of manufacturers now ship their guitars tuned to standard pitch, it's not a bad idea to loosen the strings. This is not because the guitar is in danger in an unpressurized cargo space at 30,000 feet, but because when guitars get thrown around or dropped while in the case, the peghead often cracks around the nut, sort of a whiplash injury. Loosening the strings *and* packing the neck and peghead within the case so they cannot move is cheap insurance against the most common type of damage to guitars in transit, whether by airplane or oxcart.

13. *Old guitars sound better than new ones.*

Most everyone agrees that a good guitar's tone and volume improve with time, and theories abound as to why and how it happens. Regardless of how it happens, be careful about translating this into meaning that old guitars are inherently superior to new ones. Also remember that improvements gained during the breaking-in period have to level off eventually. You don't want to overlook a good guitar on its way to greatness in favor of an older guitar that is already at its best.

14. *The best Martins were made before the company lost all its best wood in a fire.*

There are probably more myths about the Martin Guitar Co. than about all the other acoustic guitar makers in North America combined. Mike Longworth, Martin's historian and public relations man for almost 30 years, once said: "Pick any year you like, and that's when Martin either had a fire or the company was bought out by the Japanese, or both." The worst fire at Martin only scorched one or two guitar bodies. Most of the "best wood lost in a fire" myths are a result of Martin's switch from Brazilian rosewood to east Indian rosewood in 1969, but this change had nothing to do with a fire.

15. *Handmade guitars sound better than factory-made guitars.*

At the risk of being booed loudly at the next luthiers' convention, I think this is another myth. For one thing, the terms *handmade* and *factory-made* can be quite misleading. Many independent guitar makers who work alone use as many jigs, fixtures, and power tools as the big manufacturers. Is using a router the same as using a chisel? OK, what if the router is controlled by a computer? If one person works alone, making all the decisions and completing all the steps in building a guitar, but uses a computer-numerically-controlled (CNC) machine to shape all the parts, is the result still a handmade guitar? Factory guitars today are probably better than ever before, and independent builders, at least in the U.S., are far more "jigged up" than in the past, blurring the distinctions between "handmade" and "factory-made" guitars. The bottom line is that you can't generalize about the quality of an instrument by the type of shop in which it was made; use your hands, ears, and eyes instead.

The worst fire at Martin only scorched one or two guitar bodies.

A Guide to Steel and Nylon Strings

Harry Fleishman

With few exceptions, all guitar players must change their strings sooner or later. Of course, there are a couple of rasping twangers who swear by their original strings, but what they may save for buying beer, they lose in signal-to-noise ratio and sweetness of tone. Most of us enjoy the pleasures of new strings (like new socks) and only wish they were easier to choose, put on, and keep in tune.

After about 20 years of building and repairing guitars, searching constantly for the best strings to put on my instruments, I am pleased to say that we guitarists and luthiers have more good strings to choose from than ever—strings that provide longevity as well as excellent tone. The abundance of choices can make it more difficult to know what you like and how to find it, however. Do you like brass or bronze, phosphor or 80/20? Do you need high-tension classicals or low-tension folk? Is that wound third string right for you? Medium or light, smoking or nonsmoking?

A little information about how strings are made should help clear up some of the mysteries surrounding strings. The more you know about your strings and their upkeep, the better your guitar will sound.

GAUGES, TENSION, AND ALLOYS

Whether you play concert-hall classical guitar or beer-hall slide guitar, the type of strings you choose will have a significant effect on the sound you produce. The gauge-to-pitch ratio, the alloy employed, and the relationship of the core to the wrapped wire determine how a string will sound. Most guitars are strung with either steel strings or nylon strings. And although you may play a "steel-string guitar," odds are that you use either bronze-wound strings or brass strings. Some players, however, do use steel strings: steel wire wrapped on a steel core. There are also hybrids, such as strings with a nylon wrap over the wire and silk-and-steel (bronze) strings. There are nearly as many nylon string variations available as there are steel strings.

The gauge of string chosen for a given pitch will determine how much mass there is to excite the top of your guitar. Heavier strings can move the top more than lighter strings can, up to a point; if the strings are *too* heavy, they can actually restrict the top's motion. It is a case of wasted energy and a potential case of guitar abuse. An average set of light-gauge steel strings pulls on the top with a total of 150–165 pounds, silk-and-steels pull within the neighborhood of 125 to 130 pounds, and heavies are way up in the range of 200–225 pounds. Individually the difference is more subtle, but it adds up. A light-gauge .032-inch D string pulls around 30 pounds, and a medium-gauge .035 raises the tension to over 35.5 pounds (based on D'Addario phosphor-bronze strings on a guitar with a 25.5-inch scale length).

Classical strings put considerably less tension on the guitar. Normal-tension strings have between 75 and 85 pounds of pull, and hard tension around 5 pounds more. Clearly, putting steel strings on a classical guitar is bound to cause trouble. On the other hand, classical strings, while not dangerous to a steel-string guitar, will not provide enough tension to sufficiently activate the top. Some classical string makers have experimented with a high-density nylon that was developed for deep-sea fishing. The resulting string is much smaller in gauge and provides extremely high tension.

I wish I could suggest a rule of thumb to help when choosing string gauges. It would save everyone a lot of time and money. However, even the string makers acknowledge that strings are a very personal matter. Representatives from each of the major string manufacturers I spoke with agreed that all the premium strings available today are very good. But each of us hears differently, and each string is subtly different.

All that said, there are a couple of guidelines you can follow. If you play a small-bodied or delicately built guitar, avoid medium and heavy strings. Some guitar companies even stamp it in their instruments: "Use medium-gauge or lighter strings only." Kit Simon, of

---

COMPARING BRONZE STRINGS

Q *What are the differences between the acoustic bronze strings sold by various manufacturers?*

A The major differences between bronze strings are the alloys used in the windings, the size of the windings and core wire within each string gauge, and the quality controls applied to the string during manufacture. There is no bronze in any bronze strings. The core is high-tensile steel music wire (very strong, stretchy, and uniform wire), and the overspun winding wire is a brass alloy.

Originally the windings of all bronze strings were made from a relatively soft yellow brass alloy. In recent years, many people have changed to reddish-brown phosphor-bronze strings, which are believed to improve the sound of the guitar and stay bright longer. Phosphor-bronze is an alloy that is simply denser and harder than the others. Thus, at any given diameter and open pitch, a phosphor-wound string's mass is greater, and thus its tension is greater. More tension results in more sound output. So be aware that when you install a set of light-gauge phosphor-bronze strings you are in fact putting on something like light-and-a-quarter. Indeed, if you've recently turned to phosphor-bronze mediums, you may be putting more strain on your guitar than you ought to; keep an eye out for any progressive soundboard distortion.

—*William R. Cumpiano*

TYPICAL STRING GAUGES

The following chart shows typical gauges for sets of acoustic steel strings. Actual gauges and designations may vary between manufacturers; medium-light sets (with medium bass strings and light trebles), for example, are marketed under many names. Also note that true heavy sets are rarely found, making mediums about the heaviest most players will use for standard tuning.

	First	Second	Third	Fourth	Fifth	Sixth
Ultra Light	.010	.014	.022	.030	.039	.047
Extra Light	.011	.015	.023	.032	.042	.050
Light	.012	.016	.024	.032	.042	.054
Medium-Light	.012	.016	.025	.035	.045	.056
Medium	.013	.017	.026	.035	.045	.056
Heavy	.014	.018	.027	.039	.049	.059

the Olde Town Pickin' Parlor in Arvada, Colorado, tells me that when players ask his advice, he suggests a few ideas. "If it's an old guitar or a cheap guitar, I tell them to start with lighter strings." He also asks how experienced they are. "A less experienced player might want a lighter string." Ultra-light strings are probably only appropriate for players who bend strings dramatically. They have little mass and thus produce lower volume and less tone. However, they do allow electric players to get around more easily on acoustic guitars. As your fingers toughen up and you learn what your guitar can deal with, you can go up in tension; till then, it's good to play it safe. And remember that a heavier string will not necessarily sound louder or better. Some instruments, turn-of-the-century guitars for example, shouldn't be strung with anything heavier than silk-and-steels. These are a tad heavier than most extra-light strings but generally pose no threat to lightly constructed guitars. Lightly braced guitars and small-bodied guitars often respond best to light and even extra-light strings. The reduced tension of these strings won't be much good for hard-played bluegrass, but it will allow a lighter guitar to express itself over a greater range of subtle dynamics.

Just as light gauges offer a range of dynamics at the quieter end of the spectrum, providing good full tone from the lighter guitar, heavy strings provide greater volume from a big guitar that can take their greater tension. Dreadnoughts tend to take well to mediums. If you play hard, try either a bluegrass gauge, with its lighter trebles, or true mediums. Keep an eye on your bridge and neck, however. If they show any signs of trouble, go to lighter strings and have the problem looked into by a qualified repairperson.

In classical guitar strings, there's more to look out for in addition to gauge variations. There are also varieties of windings and materials that can have a profound effect on tone. In a typical string set, the top three are plain and the bottom three are wound, but some companies offer wound second and third (B and G) strings as well as the occasional wound first (E). Although these strings cause much more finger noise than plain nylon, they also have brighter timbre and more volume.

Most players assume that the alloy from which a string is made determines its tone. While this is largely true, it is an oversimplification. Brass is a commonly used alloy for guitar strings; most of the strings called "bronze" are actually brass. Brass is an alloy of copper and zinc; bronze is an alloy of copper and tin. A string designated as 80/20 bronze is actually brass: 80 percent copper and 20 percent zinc. Some of the bright bronze or bright brass strings are 60 percent copper and 40 percent zinc. Phosphor-bronze is a copper-tin-phosphor alloy that has been used successfully for many years. Phosphor-bronze strings are usually 90 percent copper and 10 percent tin, with a pinch of phosphorous for added life.

When I began researching guitar strings, I assumed that all other things being equal, bronze strings would sound one way, brass strings another. But as it turns out, all other things are never equal. At least as important as the alloy used to make a string is the relationship between the core diameter and the winding diameter. Some manufacturers use a larger core and a smaller winding, some the opposite, and some insist that the core and

NYLON STRING TENSION

Q *How do I choose among the different tensions available for nylon strings?*

A Unlike steel strings, which are labeled by gauge, nylon strings are categorized by tension, ranging from extra low to extra high. The right set of nylon strings will depend on the instrument they're being used with as well as the feel and sound you're looking for. A guitar with a very lightly braced, ultra-thin top will most likely sound better with low-tension strings, while one that's built heavier may need higher string tension to drive the top efficiently. A low-tension set will offer easier playability than a tighter set, and players with a heavy right-hand attack are likely to prefer a harder tension than those who pick softly. Experimentation is the key to finding the ideal set for you and your guitar, and with very few exceptions, a high-tension set won't damage an instrument optimized for a lighter set.

Few steel-string pickers would think about going through the trouble of selecting individual bass and treble strings from different manufacturers, but this is a common practice among serious nylon-string players. The reason for this is the greater difference between the wound bass strings (which consist of thin metal wire wound around a nylon filament core) and the plain trebles (which are solid nylon). For example, some trebles are thinner in diameter than others, and some companies (including Savarez) offer sets with wound second and third strings, which can really help with volume and tone.

Many nylon-string players change their bass strings more frequently than they do their trebles, and some even say that the trebles sound better as the material hardens with age. D'Addario is one of several manufacturers that offer specially packaged sets with extra basses for this purpose.
—*Teja Gerken*

winding must be the same diameter for maximum brightness. There's no clear consensus about what combination results in what sound, but many string manufacturers feel that a smaller core and a larger wind produce brighter, more flexible strings, and that, conversely, a larger core produces a louder, more durable string with greater sustain. Each company has a slightly different way of winding strings, but each must choose the core diameter and winding diameter to achieve a given gauge and timbre. Unfortunately, the core-to-wrap ratios used by the different string makers are seldom available to the public.

Speaking of cores, it is the core of a silk-and-steel string that is silk and steel, not the wrap—and it's actually a nylon filament, or floss, combined with steel. This combination allows the string to have enough mass to provide good sound, with a considerably lower tension at the core to protect the instrument and make it easier to play. The wrap, which is either brass or bronze, provides the timbral variation. The bronze-wound strings are mellower, in general, than the brass-wound silk-and-steels, which are treated with a silver-coated copper alloy.

A few companies offer coated strings. Many years ago one company produced nylon-wrapped acoustic strings that offered a soft, gentle sound with very little finger noise. It didn't catch on with enough players to stay on the market. The Maxima Gold company makes gold-plated strings for both acoustics and electrics. They are quite expensive, as one would expect, but also very long-lasting, impervious as they are to oxidation. Elixir strings, which are manufactured by W.L. Gore and coated with a special polymer, are becoming more and more popular among players. They're easy on the fingers, and they last for a long, long time.

Everyone has his or her own preferences when it comes to strings. Kit Simon finds that fingerstyle players tend to like brighter strings, which offer a bit more definition. He likes phosphor-bronze strings, though, for their longer life. GHS offers a chart comparing the brightness of its strings, with the bright bronze at one end of the scale and silk-and-bronze at the other. The company emphasizes, however, that each manufacturer's strings will be a little different and that the chart only applies to GHS strings. It's a start. If each company could give us a few reference points, it would help.

STRINGING A CLASSICAL WITH STEEL

Q *Can you put nylon strings on a steel-string without damaging the guitar?*

A Putting nylon strings on a guitar that is designed for steel-strings won't do any harm, but there are several factors to consider. Unless your guitar has a pinless bridge, you will have to use strings equipped with ball ends, such as D'Addario Folk Nylons or La Bella Folksingers. Furthermore, the treble slots of the nut will have to be enlarged to accommodate the thicker strings. Other necessary adjustments may include loosening the truss rod to straighten a neck that is back-bowed due to the lower string tension.

Most guitars that were designed for steel strings end up sounding bad when strung with nylon strings because they lack sufficient tension for the top to move properly. Some saddle-mounted pickups may also produce problematic results on such instruments, as they are designed for the stronger downward pressure of steel strings. Unless your guitar has a wider-than-usual neck, you might also find that the string spacing feels uncomfortably narrow when you use thicker strings.

If you are looking for greater ease of playing, I would recommend that you try silk-and-steel strings. These combine the qualities of nylon-string basses with the trebles of an extra-light steel-string set. If you are switching from a standard set of light-gauge strings, you probably won't need any modifications to your guitar, except for a possible truss rod adjustment.

—*Teja Gerken*

MAN VERSUS MACHINE

The process of making strings is a bit of a mystery to most guitarists, and this has led to some interesting marketing. Ray Rotchlisberger of Kaman Strings describes the string-making process about as simply as it can be put: "All wound guitar strings are basically just one wire wrapped around another wire." In the old days, all guitar strings were more or less handmade. The core wire was spun in a sort of lathe, while the winder held the wrap wire in a glove, often dragging it behind his or her back for tension while stretching it taut over the spinning core. Few string manufacturers still do it this way, but there are some custom winders who do. Some fairly large manufacturers still describe their strings as handmade, although most larger string companies use computerized, automated

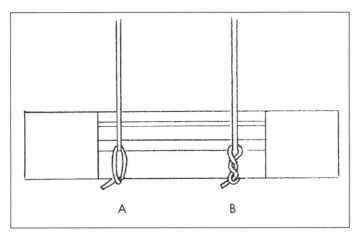

Figures A and B show two methods of tying classical guitar strings to the bridge.

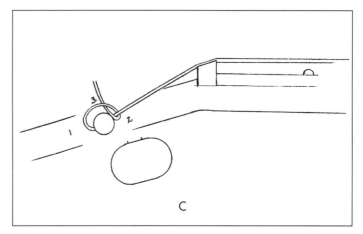

Figure C shows a step-by-step approach to securing the string to the tuning post without actually knotting it.

machinery to make strings now. In the middle are companies that use machines to wind the strings and people to monitor and adjust the process.

Everyone I spoke to in the industry agreed that the key to good strings that will last is high-quality material consistently wound, either by hand or by machine. Some acknowledged that the machines' big advantage, aside from cost, is consistent pressure. A person may pull a tauter string in the morning than in the evening, and perhaps on Friday the wind could be a bit loose. On the other hand, a person might spot a problem with the material or the wind and adjust it, while a computer might miss it. Clearly, there are advantages to each method.

PACKAGE DEAL

The finishing and packaging of strings are also interesting. For years, most companies dipped or washed their strings in an acidic bath to remove oxidation before packaging. This process involved toxic, environmentally unsound chemicals. Most, if not all, companies have stopped this procedure, and everyone I spoke with agreed that the washing was purely cosmetic and had no effect on the tone of the string. One company admitted that it had ruined some strings over the years by overwashing them and eroding some metal.

Strings are also being packaged differently than they were in the past. The D'Addario company introduced environmental packaging that uses 75 percent less material than the standard packaging (one string in each little pack, with the whole set in a plastic pouch). It's a cardboard envelope with a single plastic bag containing all six color-coded strings. The only advantage to the standard packaging that D'Addario's Steve Maroney could come up with is that some musicians might have difficulty distinguishing one gauge from another when changing strings on a dark stage. Of course, it's easy enough to bypass this problem by keeping a couple of old string packs around and reloading them from environmental packs.

One cautionary tale related to string packaging: For a couple of years I felt that a certain string clearly sounded better than its nearest competitor. The two brands were very close in tone and feel, but I liked one better. I used my second favorite for set-

WHEN TO CHANGE STRINGS

Q *How often should I change strings?*

A There is no definitive answer to this question. In order for a string to be in tune with itself, it has to have the same mass and flexibility along its entire vibrating length. As strings age, they get loaded up unevenly with dirt, hand oils, and acids, and they also suffer from metal fatigue. These factors make the strings vibrate unevenly, making tuning a nightmare. So, you should pay attention to the tunability of your instrument; when it gets hard to tune, it may be time to change strings.

Many of my customers change strings every other gig to get full brightness; some change every day, particularly if they are in the studio. The answer is subjective with regard to tone; if you like that new string sound, you had better get a string company endorsement or be prepared to spend all your lunch money on strings. I generally change strings after about 15 playing hours or at the point at which intonation starts getting weird.

—*Rick Turner*

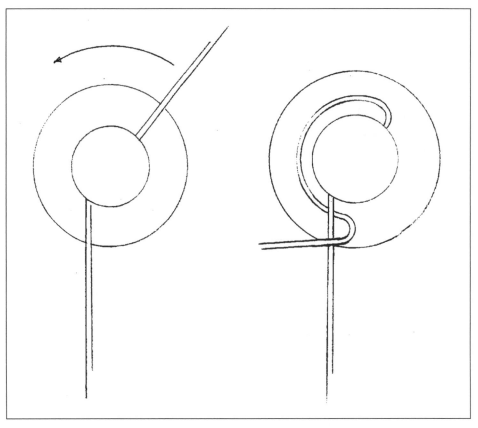

To secure a steel string to its post, pull it through and loop it under and around itself. The fewer wraps, the better.

TUNING UP

Q *What is the best way to tune my strings?*

A To get into standard tuning (E A D G B E, low to high), start by using a tuning fork or electronic tuner to get a true E note. Tighten or loosen the sixth string until it matches the E pitch. Then fret it at the fifth fret and match that pitch to the adjacent (fifth) string. Use the same method to tune the fourth and third strings. To tune the second string, fret the third string at the fourth fret and match that tone to the open second string. Then tune the first string by matching the pitch to the fifth fret of the second string. You may need to go back and tweak some of the strings once you have all of the strings close to pitch. Check the low E against the high E, the open D string against the B string fretted at the third fret, and the open A string against the G string fretted at the second fret.

—*Simone Solondz*

ting up guitars as I built them, and my favorite when I shipped the guitar to the customer. I always recommended my favorites, in spite of their higher cost, until I found out that both strings are made by the same company, using the same alloy, the same core-to-wrap ratio, and the same gauges. Apparently what I preferred was the name, the package, or the ads.

STRINGS ATTACHED

The way you put on your strings can have a profound effect on the way they perform. I had a customer who pulled the strings out of the package, yanked them open and stretched them like taffy between his hands, and then wondered why they wouldn't play in tune. He was putting little kinks in the strings that made them vibrate unevenly. Once he recognized the problem, he gently unwrapped and uncoiled his strings, and his troubles were over. Well, except for getting gigs.

Stringing a standard steel-string guitar is relatively simple. Most good guitars have at least a 14-degree downward angle from the body to the peghead. This is sufficient to allow stringing with a single wrap on the machine. Contrary to some old tales, the fewer wraps the better. This provides less opportunity for slipping and stretching. Of course this also means you must lock the string somehow. The illustration above shows an easy and effective method for securing the string at the post. Simply pull the string through the post and loop it under and around itself so that when brought up to tension, it is holding itself down against the post.

Guitars with slotted pegheads are a bit more difficult to string. The illustration on page 33 shows a couple of different ways to tie a classical string at the bridge. Figure A shows an elegant, simple solution, but some players prefer the more secure method shown in Figure B. Figure C shows the sequence of moves needed to secure the string onto the post without actually knotting it. First, pull the string through the post. Second, loop it under and around, like the steel-string method. This makes restringing quick and easy. For added security (step three), pull the string through its own loop.

Some steel-string guitars have new, self-locking tuning machines. I prefer them for several reasons. First, they are very quick when changing strings: no tying, no stretching. Second, with locking machines you never need to wrap the string on the post; I use less than one full wrap, and there's very little stretching once the strings are on and tuned. Several companies make good-quality locking tuners. Some lock with a knob on the back, while others actually lock as you tighten the string. If you are thinking of changing machines, perhaps to replace worn-out tuners, look into these at your local guitar shop. Be sure that your repairperson is qualified, however, before he or she starts drilling and reaming your guitar's peghead. All tuning machines must be carefully installed to operate properly. If your strings are constantly going out of tune, improperly installed, loose tuning machines might be to blame. Also keep in mind that replacing tuners on a vintage instrument could affect its value.

CARE AND FEEDING

Guitar strings will live longer and sound better if you take good care of them. They should have fresh food and water twice a day. Wait, that's puppies. They should be wiped off after each playing session, however brief. Some guitarists use wiping cloths impregnated with lubricants or anti-oxidants. If you have acidic sweat (you know who you are; you kill strings instantly no matter how often you wash your hands), this might just buy you a little more life from your strings.

If your budget is really tiny, you might try boiling your strings to get an extra night or two out of them. This removes the grunge, allowing them to vibrate more freely. Unfortunately, it doesn't affect metal fatigue, however, a more common and problematic cause of dead strings.

Some guitarists like to change their strings daily, some never. I have played with a classical performer who changed strings before every concert. That was one kind of nightmare to me: installing, stretching, and tuning a brand-new set of classical strings and then performing on them. One of my customers, who plays a guitar I made for him about 15 years ago, has never put a complete set on his guitar since I delivered it. He changes strings when they break! And then, only the one that broke. Another nightmare, in my book.

I know guitarists who kill strings just by looking at them and others who get months out of a single set. Don't feel bad if you're in the former group or smug if you're in the latter. It is not a reflection on you as a person.

When changing a string, a gentle tug at about the 12th fret before tuning it all the way up to pitch is enough to prove that it is not going anywhere and will also help it stay in

STICKING BRIDGE PINS

Q *How can I remove bridge pins that are stuck in my guitar? Or, conversely, what should I do if they keep popping up when I bring the strings up to pitch?*

A Most string winders include a tool designed specifically for removing stubborn bridge pins. You could also try using needle-nose pliers to *gently* pull on the pin, but be very careful not to mark the wooden bridge or the pin itself. Another technique (which also works if the top of the pin has broken off) is to reach inside the guitar through the soundhole and push the pin out with a flat object such as a quarter.

If you frequently encounter this problem, it may be an indication that something is wrong with your guitar. Perhaps high humidity has caused your bridge and/or bridge pins to swell. Dropping a couple of silica packs into your case to absorb the extra moisture will solve this problem. Another possibility is that your bridge is lifting. Try pushing a piece of paper under the bridge; if it slips in between the bridge and the top, you'll need to have a professional reglue it. Finally, the bridge plate inside the guitar could be worn. This could cause the ball ends to get jammed into the pins, thereby effectively locking them in position.

If, on the other hand, your bridge pins keep lifting out, try putting a little kink in the string just above the ball-end before inserting it. This will keep the ball-end from getting stuck at the tip of the bridge pin, which is what causes the pin to lift.

—Teja Gerken

tune. Stretch the string again after tuning up to pitch and repeat the process five or six times to stabilize the tuning on your steel-string. Nylon strings—particularly the trebles—may take several days to stabilize, so it's best to wait a couple of days between changing strings and performing or recording with a nylon-string guitar. Many classical players change bass strings much more frequently than they change their trebles.

Strings can either be changed one at a time or in one fell swoop. Changing them one at a time makes it easier to get back into tune, and if your guitar has any loose parts—such as archtop bridges, nuts, and saddles—that are held in place by string tension, the one-at-a-time method will keep them from falling off. Changing all the strings at once tends to be a lot faster, however, and allows you to thoroughly clean the fingerboard each time you change strings.

Try many different gauges and alloys from different companies until you find the right strings for you. Then try others as time goes on and your tastes change. There are lots of good strings on the market, and each set is a bit different. A little experimentation can really pay off: the right string can improve your sound *and* your performance.

RESONATOR GUITAR STRINGS

Q *What kind of strings, and what gauges, should I use on my round-neck resonator guitar?*

A Whether they have cone resonators (like Nationals) or spider-type resonators (like most Dobros), resophonic instruments deliver optimal tone and volume with minimal buzz and rattle when the strings exert sufficient downward pressure on the bridge-resonator assembly. Since these guitars have relatively shallow neck-to-body angles and a fairly low rake from bridge to tailpiece, most players favor strings of medium or heavy gauges. I use a custom-made set of heavy-gauge, brass-wound, round-core strings: .016, .018, .029, .036, .048, .060. The brass winding stops short of the tailpiece and is replaced by a light silk wrap to maximize pressure on the bridge. This improves the guitar's sound and keeps the low string from popping out of the saddle slot.

Many of my favorite players, notably Bob Brozman, favor beefed-up string gauges, but some guitarists find them difficult to negotiate manually. Marie Nordlinger at National Reso-Phonic told me that new guitars leave the shop fitted with medium-gauge (.013–.056) bronze-wound strings by John Pearse. Maestro John Hammond uses a similar set on his old Style O but subs a .014 for the first string and an unwound .026 for the third. Boston blues boss Paul Rishell strings his contemporary National polychrome tricone with a light-gauge (.012–.053) D'Addario bronze set! He shims the nut to cut down on buzz and amplifies the guitar to increase its volume. Some resophonic players still opine that a more "authentic" sound can be attained by using nickel-wound strings.

Not knowing the model or condition of your guitar, or what styles of music interest you most, I'd suggest you experiment while adhering to the heavier-is-better principle. Remember that on all guitars of this type, the resonator is held in place by string tension, so it's best to change your strings two or three at a time rather than removing the entire set at once.

—Steve James

Guitar Care Basics

Simone Solondz

Over the years, you've heard all kinds of conflicting advice about how to take care of your acoustic guitar. You've heard stories of guitarists who ruined their axes by not loosening the strings properly before traveling, by hanging it by the headstock, or by leaving it out in the sun. Which stories are true and which are urban myths? Where can you draw the line between responsible ownership and maniacal overprotectiveness?

Let's start by trying to learn from the mistakes that other guitar owners frequently make. I spoke to some of the country's best repairers to find out where guitar players tend to go wrong. Dan Erlewine, of Stewart-MacDonald fame, says, "The biggest problem I see with acoustic guitars in need of repair is that someone has tried a home remedy. Then it's not a repair; it's a restoration. The most common problems have to do with bridges and bridge reinforcing plates, interior bracing, and cracks of all kinds that were not repaired correctly or were repaired with the wrong type of glue. Do not glue anything on your guitar! Take it to a professional whose references you've checked."

Bryan Galloup, who runs Bryan Galloup's Guitar Hospital in Big Rapids, Michigan, concurs and adds that he sees botched home repair jobs where players have actually used wood screws to secure a lifting bridge. "We see woodworking screws holding the bridge down that are screwed right down into the brace! There's a top brace that travels directly underneath where it looks like the screws should go."

So, if you own a decent guitar (and especially if you own a good guitar or a collectible guitar!), don't try to do your own repair work. Luthiers have years and years of experience dealing with exactly the kinds of problems your guitar is going to encounter. Even if you're good with your hands and build your own wood furniture, don't try to apply your skills to that D-18. The tools are different, the techniques are different, and the finish is different.

Assuming that your guitar is currently in good shape, let's assess the places it hangs out—your house, your car, the local coffeehouse—and try to determine where and how it's likely to get damaged. Probably the first thing you'll want to think about is temperature and humidity. Most acoustic guitars are built of wood, which responds dramatically to changes in climate. If you want to keep your guitar consistently playable, you'll need to

Beware of the power of the great guitar killer in the sky.

store it in a somewhat consistent climate. You won't need to install a professional climate-control system, such as the ones most guitar builders use in their shops; you'll just need to use some common sense. In the dead of winter when the heater is blasting, you'll need to think about humidifying your guitar. If you're driving down to your brother's place in Florida, you should expect your ax to take a few days to acclimatize itself. And you need to be sensible about where you keep your guitar: indoors, not outdoors; not in an icy attic or a damp garage; and not on top of a heating vent or next to a radiator. "When it comes to the acoustic guitar, humidity is the main thing we're battling," says Galloup. "Over time, your guitar slowly dries out. It will eventually crack, and the glue joints will slip. You've got to put a soundhole humidifier in there and keep it in the case during the winter when the heater is on." Renowned repairman Flip Scipio points out that you must be especially careful about leaving a black guitar in front of a window where the sun is shining in because it will heat up incredibly quickly. (The effects of heat and humidity, as well as many other subjects raised in this chapter, are discussed in full detail elsewhere in this book.)

The next most common way that guitars get damaged is just by getting bumped, knocked over, sat upon, or otherwise "oopsed." "Stupid stuff happens all the time. People step on the cord while the guitar is still plugged in and it falls over," says Scipio. "The typical broken guitar is generally a drunken situation," says Galloup. "And guitar stands are a definite culprit. I view them as one of my biggest money makers. They fall forward, and that's an automatic break." Storing your guitar in a closed, hard-shell case under the bed is certainly one way to keep it safe, but it might also keep you from playing every day. Your best bet is to buy a solid, stable guitar stand and keep it in a safe, out-of-the-way corner. Stands are inexpensive and they come in a wide variety of styles. You can also get one that mounts to the wall or attaches to a bookcase or other piece of heavy furniture. *Don't* lean your guitar against the wall where it's likely to fall over, or hang it on a hook that's attached precariously to the wall. If you do want to put your guitar away for a while, use the case and put it somewhere sensible: not on a high closet shelf or under a convertible couch where it might get flattened the next time you have an overnight guest. And be sure to close the latches when your guitar is in the case. The last thing you want is for your spouse to pick up the case to sweep underneath it only to have your precious guitar come clattering out onto the tile floor!

OUT OF THE HOUSE

Once you're confident that your guitar is safe at home, think about other places it goes and how it gets there. If you're taking your guitar out, always carry it in a case or well-padded gig bag. Make sure that the case is closed and that the strap is secure before you pick it up. Cheap, flimsy gig bags can really be dangerous. Scipio tells the all-too-common tale of the customer who makes an appointment to bring his guitar in for a minor repair like a bridge reglue or tuner replacement, packs it in a gig bag, arrives at the shop, and opens the bag only to be faced with a nice, new crack.

"The broken peghead is also common," says Galloup. "It's a way of life with mahogany-neck guitars." Remember to loosen the strings if you're traveling far, and always pad the area around the guitar's peghead with T-shirts or other soft cloths. If the case does get bumped or dropped, this padding will keep the peghead from splitting off the neck. Treat your guitar more like a fellow passenger than a piece of luggage when possible. Put it in the back seat of your car rather than in the trunk if there's room. If it has to go in the trunk, get it out of there the minute you get to where you're going. Even if you park in the shade, on a hot day your trunk can become an oven, and in the hour that it takes to eat your lunch or do your errands, your guitar can undergo serious damage. If you're traveling by train or by bus, try to find a safe spot near your seat to stow your guitar, rather than trusting it to baggage handlers and other passengers.

If you're flying with your guitar, there's a good chance that the airline will force you to check it. If you've packed it in a small, soft gig bag, you might be able to fit it into the overhead compartment inside the plane, but if the staff refuses to let you bring it on board, your ax may be in danger. It's better to be safe and go to the airport with a heavy-duty, hard-shell case. You can still ask to gate-check your guitar, which means that you carry it right up to the plane. And most airlines now unload guitars at the large baggage area (where you pick up pets in cages and such) rather than throwing them on the conveyor belt where they might get squished between two huge suitcases.

Be sensible about where you take your guitar. If you play an old flattop you bought for $100, sure, take it to the beach and have fun. But if you own a vintage D-18, play

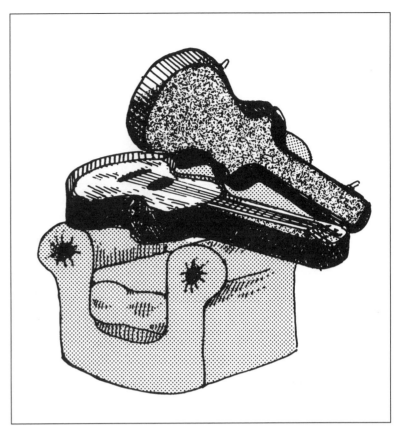

Armchairs make good, safe guitar perches around the house.

someone else's guitar around the campfire or buy yourself a cheap beater for playing out. Even if your ax is fully insured, you'll kick yourself if something happens to it, and there's no sense tempting fate.

Once you get to where you're going, you need to keep a careful eye on your guitar. It will be exposed to dangers it never faced at home: your sister's cat, who "*never* pees outside his litterbox"; the hotel maid who's come in to clear up the dishes; the club owner's teenage son who loves guitars and can't afford one of his own. . . . We hear about dozens of players losing their guitars at gigs. If you want to be safe, just keep your guitar with you rather than leaving it backstage. You don't need to upset the staff by making a big stink about possible thieves; just quietly pack up your guitar after sound check and take it with you. And when people ask if they can play your guitar, don't be afraid to say no. It's better to let friends of friends think you're a little neurotic than to go home with a big scratch on the back of your guitar from Uncle Leroy's cowboy belt.

When you get home, you may want to change your strings and give your guitar a little cleaning. Invest $3 in a guitar cleaning product and apply it to your instrument with a soft chamois cloth (you can buy just the thing at your local music store). After you've removed the strings from your guitar, use a very fine (0000-grade) steel wool to clean up the fingerboard and then rub in a tiny amount of lemon oil or mineral oil. Make sure to remove all the excess oil with a clean cloth. And remember that not all furniture polishes and waxes are appropriate for your guitar. One of the common remarks Scipio hears from customers is "The guy at the hardware store said this polish works on everything."

With a little care and common sense, your guitar should last for decades. The steps you take to protect it will of course be proportional to how much it's worth. If you own an expensive, collectible instrument, you should keep it at home in a top-of-the-line case and be extra careful about heat and humidity. If you own a great but easily replaceable guitar, there's probably no harm in taking it with you on the road, and it would be foolish to spend twice as much on a great flight case than you spent on the guitar.

Cleaning and Polishing

Frank Ford

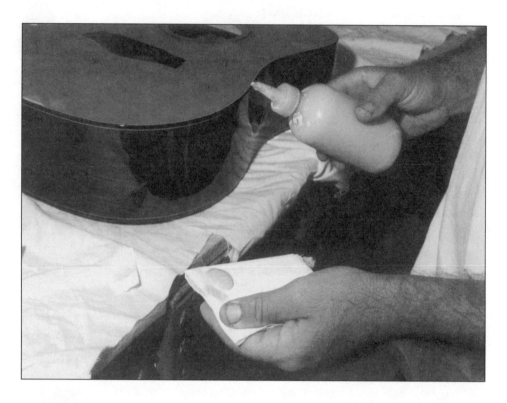

You can't play your guitar without touching it, and you can't touch it without getting it at least a little dirty. If you take a bit of time to do some "preventive cleaning" each time you play, you can avoid a number of future problems. Let's deal with the easy stuff first and then proceed to the more drastic cleaning and polishing techniques.

There's no doubt about it: a soft cotton cloth is the best thing for polishing and cleaning guitars. You can get a flannel guitar polishing cloth from your local music store and rest assured that it is safe to use on any instrument. An old 100 percent cotton T-shirt makes a great guitar wiping tool too, and the more it has been laundered the freer it will be from lint. Paper towels can actually scratch a fine guitar's finish, especially if it's lacquer or shellac French polish. If you'd like to use a disposable cloth, get the nonwoven shop towels that come on a roll or in a box. They cost about three times as much as paper towels, but they don't break down in water and they won't scratch. Each time you wipe down your guitar after playing it, you actually do a bit of polishing, too. In fact, simply wiping your guitar with a cotton cloth will keep it looking like new. Some areas may seem a bit hard to reach, such as the soundboard under the strings, but you can simply shove the cloth under there and take off the surface dust.

Speaking of strings, you can greatly extend the tonal life of strings by wiping them vigorously each time you play. Some players even wipe their strings down from time to time during a playing session. Simply grip each string through the cloth and scrub up and down the length of it. You can also keep the fingerboard relatively clean by wiping right over the board, strings and all.

As you wipe down your guitar, particularly the top and back, you may notice some spots that don't come perfectly clean. Fingerprints, smudges, and other dirt may respond well to a trace of moisture. "Huff" some warm breath on the surface the way you would if you were about to wipe the inside of your car's windshield. Just that little bit of condensation may be enough moisture to allow you to wipe the offending area clean. If you need a bit more cleaning power, try moistening the wiping cloth with a little mild detergent in water. Wet the cloth, not the guitar. That way you'll be able to control how much water actually gets on the surface. The idea is to use as little moisture as possible, to avoid getting it into any tiny voids in the finish. Follow the damp wiping by buffing with a dry cloth to remove any streaks. There are basically three types of commercial

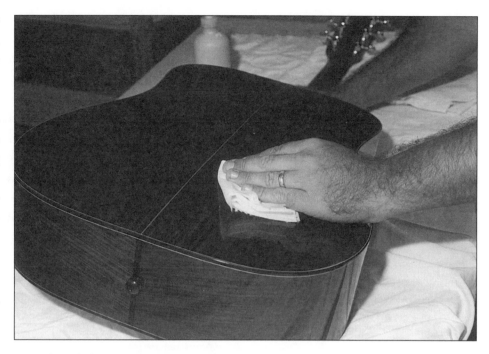

guitar polishes and cleaners on the market: water-based cleaners; creamy, water-based cleaners with very fine abrasives; and oils. Most of these are fine products, and used according to directions they will give good results.

Oils will remove oily smudges but may not have any effect on water-soluble dirt. Water-based cleaners (which look semitransparent in the bottle) should be sprayed on the cloth rather than on the instrument and will clean up water-soluble dirt best. The creamy polishes may have a slight abrasive and are best avoided if you have a matte-finished guitar. Too much polishing can cause a semigloss finish to become shiny in patches.

HEAVY-DUTY CLEANING

Well, so much for the easy stuff! How about guitars that are old, are covered in more serious grunge, or have damaged finishes? Some cleaning and polishing problems are best left to professionals, and some finishes are so damaged that there's nothing to be done.

Tape, stickers, and some self-adhesive accessories may leave a sticky residue behind when you remove them. Most of the time, water and guitar polish are ineffective in removing this kind of goo. Mineral spirits or naphtha (lighter fluid) won't injure your guitar's finish and will usually dissolve the sticky residue. Apply the solvent with a disposable cloth and turn the cloth often to avoid smearing the adhesive around the finish. A light buffing with a damp cloth should take care of any solvent streaks left behind.

As you play your guitar, dirt and oil from your hands gets mashed into the fingerboard. In fact, the fingerboard is the dirtiest part of most guitars. When you're changing strings, you have an opportunity to wipe down the fingerboard and really clean things up. (By the way, it doesn't hurt any guitar to take all the strings off at once.) If the dirt buildup is really bad, simply wiping with a damp cloth won't suffice. Get some extra-fine steel wool (grade #0000) and scrub the fingerboard gently across its surface, parallel to the frets. As you scrub, make sure you don't snag the ends of the frets! There's usually no need for cleaning agents, because the steel wool will scrape the dirt away. Some players talk of "feeding" the unfinished surface of the fingerboard with oil. Fingerboards are not actually hungry, but a light coating of oil gives them a finished and clean look. If you do choose to oil the fingerboard, do it with care. Use a tiny amount of lemon oil or mineral oil on the rag, wipe it on the fingerboard, and then wipe it all off. You don't want to saturate the fingerboard, and you don't want a lot of oil running down into the fret slots. If there are cracks in your fingerboard, consider having them filled professionally, and don't get oil in them. Generally, you'll want to stay away from linseed and other natural vegetable oils, which become sticky and gummy over time. This kind of fingerboard cleaning should be a once-a-year event at the most. Too much scrubbing and oiling can easily do more damage than good.

Lemon oil and other oils are often sold as instrument polish. They will not damage your finish. The oil cleaners tend to remove oil-soluble dirt, but it is very important to realize that oils and polishes can penetrate any little breaks in the finish and may make quite a mess over time. A guitar with cracks or a crazed finish should be approached with utmost caution. Oily polishes will leach right through the cracks in the finish and stain the surface of the wood, and the stains will bleed and become more ugly as the years go by. The creamy, white commercial guitar polishes will leave a high shine and will clean a new finish beautifully, but an old, crazed finish will absorb the polish and look like a dried out riverbed with white outlined cracks. Some creamy polishes have a tendency to build up on the surface, leaving a film behind. This film may look shiny and clean, but it may actually be somewhat likely to collect dirt and water spots. In other words, you might build up a waxy coating that requires more maintenance than the finish underneath. If you have a problem with one brand of creamy polish, try cleaning it off with a gentle detergent and water on a cloth and then switching to another brand.

CLEANING A RESONATOR GUITAR

 Should I remove the cover plate from my Dobro to keep the resonator clean of dust accumulation?

Disassembling a resonator guitar is something you want to avoid doing unless it's absolutely necessary. I change my strings two or three at a time to avoid resonator movement. A Dust Buster–type vacuum or a hair dryer can be used to remove dirt from the resonator well. If you feel like eating crumb cake in a dust storm, keep your guitar in its case!

—Steve James

WEAR AND TEAR

Very light surface scratches may often be rubbed out by hand using a variety of automotive and plastic polishing compounds. For recommendations about this sort of polish, see your local professional luthier. I'm particularly fond of Novus #2 plastic polish. It leaves a high gloss without a serious residue. Follow the #2 with the #1 spray to leave a clean, static-free surface. Deep scratches, scars, and other breaks in the finish tend to attract dirt like magnets. Polishing, either with water or oily cleaners, will rub the dirt right into the scratches. The best thing you can do is to simply wipe these areas with a dry cloth.

Modern instruments may be finished with a catalyzed polymer coating that is inert and unaffected by perspiration and skin oils. Nitrocellulose lacquer is much more reactive, however. As it is handled, the lacquer may react to your skin chemistry and become soft, increasing the rate at which it wears. After enough mileage, the simple act of playing a guitar will wear the finish off in the areas that are handled the most. The finish on the back of the neck gets the most handling of all. It goes without saying that you can't clean the finish if it's worn off! The area of the top where you rest your forearm is particularly vulnerable to softening as it reacts to your body chemistry. Like the neck finish, it wears prematurely when it becomes soft. If you notice a dull area where your arm rests on the soundboard, don't polish it too vigorously. You may have a slightly softened finish, and it would be a good idea to take your guitar to a professional luthier for some advice.

Humidity and Your Guitar

Bob Taylor

A swollen soundboard. Note the slight dip in the center where the top is glued to the tailblock and cannot rise with the rest of the top.

Fine guitars are made from solid wood that is cut very thin, so maintaining a proper humidity level is critical, not only to prevent cracking but also to maintain proper string action. When the guitar becomes too dry, the top will sink, causing the strings to drop closer to the neck and buzz. Eventually the guitar may develop cracks. When the guitar becomes too wet, the wood can swell tremendously, causing glue joints to fail and neck angles to go bad. Distortions in the wood may remain after the guitar is repaired, leaving the guitar cosmetically disfigured.

Your guitar will "report" its own humidity condition, and you can learn how to read this report with practice. Your guitar's case is its best protection from low humidity levels, but in areas of severe dryness you may need to humidify your instrument by using a soundhole humidifier. Be careful not to over-humidify your guitar, however. If your guitar does get too wet, a silica gel pack placed inside the case can absorb moisture.

Humidity is moisture in the air, moisture that is usually invisible. Relative humidity (RH) is the amount of moisture, measured as a percentage, that a given volume of air is capable of holding. So if the RH is measured at 30 percent, the air is holding 30 percent of what it is capable of holding. As air temperature rises, the air is capable of holding more moisture. So if you raise the temperature of a building, as you will in the winter, the RH inside the building will drop. The only way to bring the RH back up is to add moisture to the air, a task that a humidifier performs.

A lot of us only need to worry about low humidity levels in winter, when we're heating our homes, but many places have naturally low humidity all year long. The entire Rocky Mountain region is very low in humidity, as are desert cities like Phoenix, Reno, Las Vegas, and Tucson. You are most likely aware of the humidity levels in your hometown, but you may not be aware of how they affect your guitar.

A swollen back dips in the center where it is glued to the tailblock.

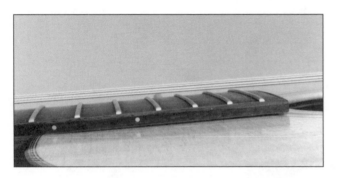

The top and fingerboard are both so swollen that the glue joint between them has failed.

WOOD AND WATER

Let's start with the basics. Guitars are made of wood, and wood is hydrophilic, meaning it loves water. Wood equalizes its moisture content to the RH that surrounds it. The moisture content of wood is not measured relative to its ability to hold water, so its values are stated in different terms than relative humidity. At 45 percent RH, wood equalizes to a moisture content of about 6 percent.

Wood cells are kind of like fat cells. (We all know about them!) Fat cells in your body never go away and are always hungry to fill themselves. Wood cells quickly gain or lose water according to the climate that surrounds them. Think of a wet guitar as a fatso and a dry guitar as an anorexic. Though only the most extreme conditions of wetness or dryness can kill your guitar, it is healthiest when the wood has the proper moisture content, just as people are healthiest at their ideal weight.

You can count on the fact that your solid-wood guitar is not magically immune to changes in humidity. Its finish (which is only applied to the outside anyway) will not stop the gain or loss of moisture. Even if your guitar was made from 25-year-old seasoned wood or built by someone really famous, it will react to humidity changes.

Simply put, when the humidity is low, your guitar dries out, causing the wood to shrink. When the humidity is high, your guitar gains moisture, causing the wood to swell. How much movement are we talking about? Most guitars are made in factories or shops controlled to about 45 percent RH. When you expose a guitar from one of these shops to 30 percent RH, the top can shrink in width by an eighth of an inch! If you take the guitar down to 15 percent RH, the top can shrink by $^3/_{16}$ of an inch. This is enough to crack the guitar's top.

Imagine that you're having a local builder make you a guitar. He's getting ready to brace your guitar and discovers that he accidentally cut the top an eighth of an inch too small. "No problem," he tells you, "I'll just use my hydraulic stretcher to pull the spruce back out until it fits and then glue it in place." You probably wouldn't buy a guitar from this birdbrain. But your guitar will undergo the same stress if you let it become too dry.

Spruce, which is often used to build tops, has a very high shrink rate, so it moves more than woods typically used for backs and sides. This is unfortunate, because every time the top shrinks or swells, it changes the guitar's neck angle and action. Wood does not shrink along its length enough to affect anything, so the guitar's braces, which are glued to its top, do not shrink and swell along with the top. Therefore, the top as a unit bows inward when dry and outward when wet. A guitar at 30 percent RH bows inward $^1/_{16}$ of an inch. When the top bows in, it takes the saddle with it, pulling the strings closer to the fretboard. This is why a guitar will tend to have low, buzzy action in the winter. When the top bows inward, the portion of the fretboard that is glued to the top also goes along for the ride, causing the 14th-fret hump that is common in dry climates. When the top bows out, the fretboard rises with it, causing extremely high action and fret buzzing in the high registers. In the most severe cases of over-humidifying, the fretboard may swell so much that it begins to separate from the top.

Many guitar owners take the advice of repairers and have their necks refretted and their saddles raised or lowered to cure these problems, when just a little drink of water or drying out will restore the guitar to its original geometry. I know it's hard to believe, but if you adjust the humidity, the top will return to its correct dimensions, the action will go back to normal, and the neck will straighten out.

RULES OF THUMB

Here are some rules to follow to keep your guitar in its best condition:

Keep your guitar stored in a good, solid case, which protects the guitar very well from humidity changes. Your solid-wood guitar is a symphony-quality musical instrument that should be cared for properly. Do not leave it out on a stand because it's beautiful or because it needs to be handy when you get a sudden inspiration. If you do insist on leaving it out, you must be sure to humidify your home properly and monitor the RH levels regularly.

Your guitar is the best humidity gauge you own, and for these purposes the only one you should trust or care about. If you look across the top of your guitar, in front of the bridge, you will notice when your top sinks in or bulges out (see photos, right). The top of your guitar should be flat or slightly swollen. If you notice it sinking in, you should also notice that your action is lower than normal and that the strings may be hitting the fretboard when you play high up the neck. The problem usually kicks in somewhere between the ninth and the 12th fret. If you notice that the top is swollen and you lay a straightedge across the lower bout, you should see a slight dip where the top is glued to the tailblock and cannot rise with the rest of the top.

You can restore the moisture to a dry guitar by placing a soundhole humidifier, such as a Damp-it, inside the guitar, closing up the guitar in its case, and leaving it for a day or so. Repeat the process until the top has returned to normal and whenever your guitar starts to display these symptoms again. Be careful not to overhumidify, and if you use a soundhole humidifier like a Damp-it, be sure to wring out the excess water before putting it in your guitar. For an overly wet guitar, you can try a similar procedure with a silica gel pack.

When shopping for a guitar, buy from stores that maintain humidity levels at 45 to 50 percent. Many new guitars are "predried" by retailers before being sold to buyers. This is not good! Sometimes people go home in the winter with brand-new guitars whose tops crack in a week, because the store didn't control its humidity and didn't talk to the customer about maintaining a proper RH at home. The guitar was on the verge of cracking when the customer bought it, and the slightest change for the worse caused the guitar to crack. Keep an eye out for guitars with sunken tops. If a shop is selling high-end guitars with sunken tops, you can bet that the inventory is not being taken care of properly. A repairer can file the frets and install a higher saddle to put a Band-Aid on the guitar, but that won't make the problem go away.

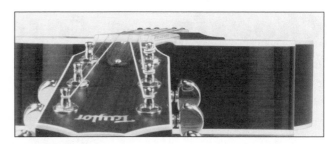

Properly humidified guitar. Neck is straight and action is correct.

Too dry. Note that the neck is bowed and the strings are lying incredibly low.

Too wet. The top is so swollen that the bridge has risen above the fingerboard.

Choosing a Case

Teja Gerken

When it comes to keeping your guitar out of harm's way, the most important decision you make will be the kind of case in which you pack it. For years, the options could be boiled down to two choices: inexpensive chipboard or more expensive plywood. Most entry-level guitars come in chipboard (essentially reinforced cardboard) cases. Although they offer basic protection, they often provide a poor fit, allowing the guitar to move around within the case. I've also seen instances where the case was too tight and, due to a lack of padding, actually wore the finish off parts of the guitar. Still, a chipboard case is better than no case, and if you're primarily concerned with storing your instrument at home or taking it to a friend's house to jam, there may not be a compelling reason to spend more money on a better case, particularly if it would exceed the value of your guitar.

Laminated plywood cases come in a wide range of quality levels. The most basic ones are made from thin, three-ply material, with flat tops and backs and minimal padding. These cases share the same traits associated with chipboard cases, although they handle impact somewhat better. A good plywood case is made of six or seven layers of wood, has an arched top and bottom (which greatly increase its ability to resist pressure), and is outfitted with thick padding and sturdy hardware. With a proper fit, this kind of case ensures excellent protection. While not as bulletproof as flight cases, good plywood cases are used by many traveling musicians and will withstand most baggage handlers. Cedar Creek, Hi-Tone, and TKL are known for high-quality wooden cases, and Ameritage even makes models with built-in humidity controls.

Nowadays, most quality guitars come in cases made of injection-molded plastic (many of which are manufactured by the SKB Corp.). These cases offer about the same amount of protec-

A host of Calton flight cases, which feature fiberglass exteriors and heavily padded interiors.

tion as good plywood models, but they weigh and cost less. Their foam interiors are molded to fit the guitar perfectly, and the foam also absorbs shock well. One of the drawbacks of most molded cases is their tendency to wear out faster than other kinds of cases. The interior foam often separates from the outer shell, and rough treatment sometimes result in cracks and dents in the exterior that are not easily fixed.

If you do a lot of traveling, you'll probably want to buy a flight case for your ax. Flight cases are made out of strong fiberglass and feature extensive padding and heavy-duty hardware. The ultimate protection is provided by cases such as those made by Anvil and Calzone, but unless you're lucky enough to have roadies, you may want to look into lighter, less bulky options. Caltons and Mark Leafs are popular flight cases.

Gig bags offer the least amount of protection from physical impact, but they are easy to carry. A huge range of quality and prices can make shopping for a gig bag a bit daunting. Cheap nylon models with flimsy zippers and almost no padding can be purchased for as little as $20, and custom-made leather bags can exceed the cost of a flight case. Pay attention to the thickness of the padding, the quality of the zipper, and the comfort of the shoulder straps. Generally, the more rigid a gig bag is, the more protection it will provide. Some inexpensive models only have one shoulder strap, making it difficult to keep them stable on your back while carrying other pieces of gear. Companies like Kaces, Levys, ProTec, and TKL make good bags at affordable prices, while Blue Heron, the Colorado Case Co., and Reunion Blues have the high-end market covered.

Another option is ProTec's ProPack, which falls somewhere between a hard-shell case and a gig bag. It features a thin plywood frame that is covered with nylon and is extensively padded. Its dimensions are a bit bigger than the standard gig bag, making it relatively bulky, but it's a good compromise between protection and comfort.

SHOPPING TIPS

When you go out to shop for a case, make sure you find one that fits your guitar snugly. Look at how the case opens and closes; the lid should not press down on any part of the guitar. Make sure all the clasps are attached firmly and work smoothly. If there's a lock, try it out to see whether it works. Put your guitar in the case and lift it up by the handle. Is it balanced? Is the handle comfortable in your hand? It may seem like an unimportant detail, but recovering from carrying a heavy case with an uncomfortable handle is the last thing you need after rushing to a gig. Some cases have hardware for attaching a shoulder strap. This is a great feature that I wish more manufacturers included.

Although I keep my own guitars in hard-shell cases at home, I use gig bags for most of my travels around town. Because it's so much easier to throw a gig bag over my shoulder than it is to schlep a heavy case, my guitar stays with me at all times and is less likely to be stolen or get damaged. With the guitar on my back, I also have both hands free to carry my amp and other gear. Of course, if you're likely to hand your guitar over to someone else or to stow it in the back of a truck with heavy equipment, you should stick with a hard-shell case. In the end, what kind of case is right for you depends on the kind of traveling you do. The more you know about what's available, the better equipped you'll be the next time you hit the road.

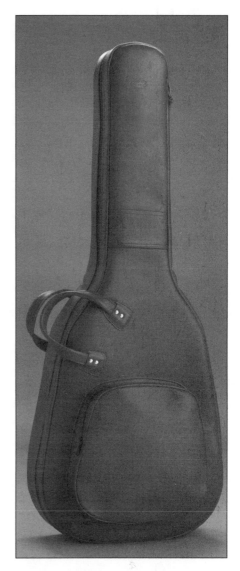

Gig bags, like this leather one from Reunion Blues, are easier to carry but offer less protection.

Flying with Your Guitar

Kristina Olsen

I am standing at the baggage claim, crowded with grumpy travelers pushing for their luggage. The conveyer belt is at an alarming angle and seems to be running way too fast. I can't make my way to the front. All of a sudden dozens of huge heavy wood crates start careening down the belt. I see my guitar dwarfed by them, and I cry out involuntarily as a particularly large crate falls on my guitar. The usually noisy baggage claim area becomes painfully silent as we all hear the horribly distinctive sound of a musical instrument, designed to transmit sound, transmitting its own death as it is reduced to splinters. I wake up in my hotel bed, a cold sweat permeating the sheets, mattress liner, mattress, and box spring. Oh thank God, it was just a dream.

How do we do it? Traveling with our beloved instruments is a nightmare. Should you check it or try to carry it on? Here are some tips to help you and your guitar survive your next flight.

CHECKING YOUR GUITAR

If you are going to check your guitar in baggage, be prepared to lose it. I have lost my guitar six times, and once it was missing for more than a month. So far I've been lucky: my guitar has always made it back to me, like those pet stories, "We lost old Sparky in Nebraska, but she caught up to us in Hong Kong." I only travel with guitars that I am emotionally prepared to lose. I can't tell you how much stress that has removed from my life.

Pad the peghead. One of the most common injuries to checked guitars is broken pegheads. Even in most good cases, the peghead is not supported. If a case is dropped, the weight of the tuning gears can snap the peghead right off. This happened to one of my guitars. Pack the peghead securely on all sides with T-shirts, socks, and other soft articles of clothing, or buy a case with padded peghead support.

Loosen the strings. On an average steel-string guitar, the strings pull 150 pounds of pressure. You won't want that kind of pressure on your guitar's neck while it is getting heaved around by sumo baggage handlers.

Choose the strongest case you can afford and/or carry. I've heard many musicians recommend Calton cases. They come in bright colors, which makes it less likely that someone will walk off with your guitar by mistake, and they have a good arch over the face of the guitar that gives the case more strength. Flight cases (usually triangle-shaped fiberglass cases) are also very good, but they are bulky and heavy. Sadly enough, I know many musicians who have developed tendon injuries not from playing their instruments but from carrying heavy cases. Generally, the heavier the case, the better the protection, so you will have to find a balance. Even the toughest cases, however, are not indestructible. One airline managed to spear a forklift right through the best case a musician friend of mine could find.

Pack your instrument and case in a cardboard shipping box. You can usually get one of these boxes for free from a music store, but you will have to get the box in advance since most stores don't get daily shipments of guitars. When I pack my guitar, I throw all my clothes and an empty duffel bag around the case for padding. The great thing about this method is that it makes your guitar so awkward and bulky that the baggage handlers have to handle it gently by default. The obvious problem with this system is that the box is awkward and bulky for you as well, and you end up taking a big empty box on tour with you for your return flight.

Once, when I wasn't using this method, I saw a baggage handler throw my guitar case over a baggage train where it landed miraculously headfirst on the conveyor belt. The baggage handler jumped up and down ecstatically at the sheer beauty and accuracy of his throw, while from inside the airplane I was screaming inaudibly and pounding on the airplane window. Of course when I checked my guitar the airline made me sign a waiver saying that any damage they inflicted on my instrument was my responsibility. Had I packed my guitar in a shipping box, I would have saved myself a $250 repair bill.

When you get to your destination, go directly to the baggage claim area to get your guitar. I once coincidentally ran into guitarist Nina Gerber as I deplaned and stood talking at the gate for ten minutes while my guitar went around and around the baggage claim carousel. Pretty soon my guitar was the only thing left, and when no one was looking someone stole it. Through some clever detective work on the part of the airline, I got my guitar back, but not until after I had played the festival.

CARRYING YOUR GUITAR ON BOARD

If you plan to try to carry your guitar on board, get a great gig bag, one that you can wear on your back. That way your guitar is pretty much hidden by your body so that when you saunter on by the ticket takers they may miss your guitar entirely. Find a bag that isn't too bulky but offers some protection. I use gig bags by Blue Heron and Reunion Blues. They use a foam similar to backpacking insulate, which is very dense and offers good protection. Gig bags don't need as much padding as regular cases because they aren't subjected to baggage handlers. And because they are so light and comfortable, you're not always setting them down, so they don't get knocked about and are less likely to get stolen.

When you make your reservation, find out what the airline's policy is for carrying guitars on board and what type of carrier the airline uses. Make sure you are not flying on an L10-11. TWA flies a lot of those. They have tiny overhead compartments that will not hold a guitar. The 700 series (e.g., 737, 747), the Airbuses, and the DC-10s are generally fine. But, whether or not there's *room* for your guitar on board, many airlines are now refusing to allow passengers to carry them on. A friend of mine used to disguise her guitar (in its gig bag) in a hanging wardrobe bag. It worked for her a few times, but now she just uses a heavy flight case and checks her guitar. In the past, I have had especially good luck with Northwest, Alaska, and Delta, but airlines are getting more strict about carry-ons all the time. When I fly overseas, I check both guitars through baggage. Most overseas carriers won't allow you to bring your guitar on board. I also have insurance for my instruments that covers airline damage and loss.

When you fly on tiny commuter planes, you will have to relinquish your guitar, but you can watch the baggage person put it in the hold yourself, and at the end of the flight you pick it up right outside the plane, so it doesn't go through the maze of conveyor belts. I have never had a problem on these little flights.

Don't push the airlines. If you are attempting to carry a guitar on board, don't bring a lot of other carry-ons. Many people have to share limited space. I have seen musicians carry on needless extra stuff and act indignant when they get called on it. A friendly positive attitude and gentle persistence will generally get you and your guitar taken care of in the best possible way.

I always fill in the customer survey cards in the in-flight magazines and tell the airline that I am flying them because they have always been great about letting me on board with my guitar in a gig bag. Airlines cater heavily to business customers, and I remind them that we musicians are business customers, too. I always try to be friendly and polite, especially if I am carrying a guitar, so that airline workers will like accommodating musicians.

Bon voyage!

Protecting Your Instrument from Theft

Jack Pearson

STOLEN!

VIOLIN

• Bust of bearded man on headpiece, coat of arms on back
• Double purfling top and back with fleur-de-lis carved in all corners
• Red flannel zipper cover in black case with octagonal bow

5-STRING BANJO

• Vega long-neck in red-lined black case
• "Man-in-the-moon" and stars neck inlays
• Brass tone ring engraved as follows:
   "THE VEGA CO. NO. A-129586 XCEL JACK
   PEARSON 1972"
• Maple resonator with riverboat scene painted on
   inside

REWARD
for information leading to recovery

ALL CONTACTS CONFIDENTIAL

**CALL COLLECT: JACK PEARSON
                MINNEAPOLIS, MN
                (XXX) XXX-XXXX**

You've just had a great gig with some fine musical moments and you're enjoying the afterglow over pie and coffee with friends. You come back to pack up your gear and look around quizzically. All at once a sickening feeling hits you in the pit of your stomach. Your guitar is gone. The one you took out a major bank loan to buy ten years ago. The one you've meticulously broken in, sweat over, loved, and worked with all these years. The one you wrote your first decent song on. Your right arm. Well, join the club. As a guy who's been there, I'd like to offer some tips to help you avoid theft in the first place and take the right steps if your instrument *is* stolen.

PREVENTION

Keep your instrument with you. This is the cardinal rule in sidestepping theft. You've all heard the story that starts, "I was only gone for a minute." But let's face it, keeping your instrument by your side is sometimes impractical. If you feel you have to leave your instrument unattended, keep in mind that some places are more dangerous than others. Airports and cars require special caution. If you must leave your guitar in your car, conceal it. I carry a blanket for the purpose.

Travel with an instrument you can emotionally and financially afford to part with. This doesn't mean you should travel with a junky guitar, but it does mean that you're asking for trouble if you lug your vintage D-28 all over the country.

Insure your instrument to as close to full replacement value as possible. It's a discouraging thing to contact your insurance company after a theft and realize that you'll only receive half the replacement value of your instrument. Guitars can and often do appreciate, so keep the insured value current. Affordable insurance rates can often be found through musical organizations or even as a rider on a homeowner policy. Some insurance companies even specialize in musical instrument coverage (see "Resources" in the back of this book).

Carry an instrument that is identifiable. The more unique your instrument is, the less likely some thief will want to risk swiping it. My fine Martin D-41S was stolen one night, but the vintage Dyer harp guitar that was sitting right next to it was left alone. The zipper bag had been opened, but the thief took one look at it and knew it was too weird to hide or sell.

This unusual scroll helped the author recover his stolen violin.

Another instrument of mine that was taken was a fancy French fiddle with a bust of Galileo for a scroll. I got it back largely because it was so unusual. A surprisingly important factor in its return was the bridge, which had the name of a violin maker in my city stamped on it. Together with an advertising effort on my part, the maker's city connected the instrument to me and led to a phone call.

If you don't want your name and phone number inlaid in big block letters on your fingerboard, you could get an outrageous-looking case. This trick has limitations though, since an instrument can easily be fenced sans case.

Write down the serial numbers of all your instruments. I also have "property of Jack Pearson" and my 800 number engraved on all my capos, one of which will quite possibly remain with my guitar should it be stolen. I also keep my business card in every case I own, with wording on the back to the effect of "If not in the possession of Jack Pearson, this instrument is stolen! Please call (phone number)." I even put one in the rosin pouch in my fiddle case! I also advise putting similar wording on a sticky label on the hidden side of the nine-volt battery in your on-board preamp, if you have one. If someone buys your stolen guitar and changes the battery, they're likely to find out that the instrument is yours. One more place you might want to contemplate including the above wording is on the X-brace on the bass side of your guitar. It's not as likely to be seen there by a right-handed person casually examining the instrument (such as the thief), but it will eventually be noticed by anyone who develops a close connection with the guitar.

THE ROAD TO RECOVERY

So you've diligently followed all the above suggestions and your Gibson SJ still gets stolen? Don't get mad, get organized! The likelihood of getting it back is directly proportional to the effort you're willing to put into recovering it (that's a direct quote from a police investigator). If you're ready to work at getting your ax back, here are some suggestions.

Time is of the essence! A thief most likely has only one interest in your instrument: quick money. He will either try to fence it right away in a somewhat distant locality or else wait for the dust to settle and try to fence it locally. My guitar was fenced the day after it was stolen at a music store about 60 miles away, though I've heard of instruments showing up at a store within blocks of the theft! So, take action, and the sooner the better.

Contact all the music stores and pawnshops within 100 miles. Get on the phone and do it now! Be sure to notify the local police as soon as possible and write down the police case number. Include this information along with a description of the instrument and the serial number when you call around. Music store staff will be sympathetic to your plight, but they're also busy, so be patient and polite. If the theft occurred near where you live, be sure to visit the music stores in person. And return every couple of weeks to check again.

Follow up all contacts with a printed piece describing the instrument that was stolen. Include a picture if at all possible (take these photos now while you still have the instrument in your possession!). I was fortunate to have a color postcard of me and my guitar. Man, did that help!

Immediately post your loss on the Web. There are a number of Web sites that will help you get the word out about your instrument. To find out about them, do a search on the Web or phone a reputable instrument dealer in your area for help.

Keep an eye on the want ads in the vicinity where the theft occurred. Believe it or not, some thieves will simply place an ad for the stuff they stole and try to sell it through the local paper! If you don't live in the area, enlist a friend to watch the ads for you.

Consider placing an ad yourself. Depending on how badly you want your instrument back, it may be worth it for you to take the further step of placing ads in national publications. This step is what brought my old French fiddle back to me—a year and a half later! This is a long-range strategy, though. Be sure to pursue immediate short-range plans first. If your instrument was taken by sophisticated thieves (which isn't likely), it may travel a long distance before being sold, which could involve quite a bit of time.

Finally, be patient, be persistent, and pray. And if worse comes to worst and the darling instrument of your heart leaves you forever, you get to embark on the exciting journey of courting and loving again! And there are more great instruments out there now than ever before. So love your instrument, but be detached, too. Make the best music you can with what you have, and remember that we live in an abundant world. And even if they take your instrument, they can never take your music!

Getting a Good Guitar Setup

Rick Turner

Adjusting the action to suit the player's needs is an important part of setting up a guitar.

Guitars, like cars and even humans, require periodic maintenance in order to perform at their very best. The most basic and common procedures performed in a guitar repair shop come under the general heading of *setup*. The term basically refers to the mechanics of setting the action and intonation. By understanding what goes into a setup, you can help guide your luthier to optimize your guitar for your style of playing and keep it at peak performance capability over the long haul.

New guitars are set up in the factory so that their tone can be evaluated, but this generic setup is rarely exactly right for a discerning player. There is no way for a luthier to know how to set up a guitar for a player he or she has never met. You don't expect the driver's seat of a new car to be adjusted perfectly for you, and you shouldn't expect the action to be perfect on your new guitar. When a luthier is setting the action at the nut or leveling the frets, the difference between just right and too low can be the thickness of a hair. To perfectly optimize these factors costs time and money beyond what factories can afford, given that they must sell at wholesale and make a profit. In my shop, a refret costs more than the wholesale price of probably 50 percent of the acoustic guitars sold in this country!

Even if they had the time, factory workers couldn't set up all their guitars "perfectly," because there is no one set of measurements or specifications that results in a correct setup for every player and every guitar. What is right for a bluegrass guitarist will certainly be wrong for a Celtic fingerstylist, and what's right for your delicate Martin New Yorker won't be right for the Gibson J-45 you use for slide. And in nylon-string guitars there's a world of difference between what's right for a classical player and a flamenco player.

Other factors that affect guitars and their setups are humidity and string tension. The vast majority of acoustic guitars are made primarily of wood, which swells and shrinks according to ambient humidity as the seasons change. Thus your guitar's setup changes with the seasons. Necks and tops gradually distort under the tension from steel strings; this distortion gradually changes the setup over the years as well. A luthier can make the normal and necessary adjustments to bring the guitar back into playability, but, to best achieve your goals as a guitarist, you need to know what is going on.

You should know exactly what you are paying for when you take your guitar in for a setup. The guitar world's definition of a setup is somewhat loose, so talk with your luthier about all the steps he or she includes. A typical setup might encompass adjusting the action at the nut and saddle, adjusting the truss rod, restringing, checking the fit of the bridge pins, and setting the intonation by filing the saddle "witness points" once action and string gauge are set. In our shop, we also clean the guitar, rub the fingerboard with lemon oil, tighten any loose tuner screws, lube the tuners (if necessary), and check the instrument for cracks, loose braces, a lifting bridge, etc. For the sake of clarity, I will not include refretting or any basic fret work (leveling, grinding, and polishing) under the heading of setup.

Before setting up your guitar, your luthier needs to know the string type and gauge you prefer, your intended playing style and tuning, and how hard you plan to play. Be clear about these factors; these are the starting parameters that determine how your guitar is set up. Also, understand that if you use a lot of tunings, your guitar will probably *not* perform equally well in all of them. Many professional musicians have guitars set up specifically for each tuning they use.

PLACING A STRAP BUTTON

Q *My guitar only has one strap button, installed on the butt of the instrument. Where is the best location to add a second pin to hold the other end of the strap?*

A I put mine on the treble side of the heel about halfway down. The guitar hangs best with the strap attached there, and in spite of what it looks like, my fretting hand never runs into it. It's not elegant or symmetrical, but it works. Some people like the button on the center of the heel, more for looks than function. That can cause problems with fitting the guitar in a case. I've also seen strap buttons in the side of the guitar on the bass side next to the heel, kind of like you'd do on a Telecaster. That's dangerous unless you reinforce the wood inside or carefully catch the neck block with the screw.

In any case, when putting in a strap button, *always* drill a pilot hole a bit smaller in diameter than the screw size. Also, beware of any bolts that might be in the heel. Modern guitar builders now consider it quite acceptable to bolt the necks on acoustic guitars, and this can cause problems for unwary strap button installers.

—*Rick Turner*

ADJUSTING THE NUT

When adjusting the action, assuming it isn't totally out of whack, I generally start at the nut. For most players, the string height at the nut should feel the same as if you placed a capo at the first fret and played up from there; the action should feel like the strings are coming off a fret. The way I set this height is to hold each string down between the second and third frets and sight for a very narrow gap between the bottom of the string and the top of the first fret. You should just be able to slip a piece of paper into that gap for the top five strings, and maybe go a bit more, say a business card, for the sixth string. This adjustment will dramatically improve the playability in 95 percent of instruments set up at the factory.

Luthiers use a variety of fine saw blades and precision needle files to make adjustments at the nut, and very fine sandpaper to polish the slots. The slots should be neither too tight, which binds the strings while you're tuning, nor too loose, which can lead to sitarlike buzzes on the open strings. The bottom of the slot itself should be a ramp closely matching the break angle of the string, and the string's point of contact should be at the fingerboard end of the slot to ensure proper intonation (see illustration below). There should be very little friction in the slots; you can lubricate them with pencil lead, wax, or Teflon grease to ease tuning woes.

When slots in the nut wear too low (or, dare I say it, are filed too low in the course of setting action), there are three basic solutions: shim up the nut with veneer, make a new nut, or fill the slot with superglue and baking soda or bone dust, and then recut the slot. The last trick works great for a few months, but must be redone after that. Of course, the old folk club trick is to put some cardboard from a matchbook under the string in the slot, but we don't do that or smoke cigarettes anymore, do we?

I sometimes raise the action at the nut a bit for bottleneck players. For Ry Cooder, I make the *tops* of the first three strings level to make for cleaner sliding. He uses his guitar for both slide and fingerstyle, so we go with a compromise setup that works for both. For a strictly slide player, I may raise the action to the point where fretting is basically impossible.

LEFTY CONVERSIONS

Q *I would like to replace the nut on my right-handed guitar with one that's cut left-handed, but I'm worried about intonation problems. What do you advise?*

A You can convert your guitar into a lefty, but you'll have to do more than change the nut. You'll also need to fill in the bridge slot and reinstall the saddle so that it's slanted the other way to compensate for intonation. This is a job for a luthier, but it falls under the heading of Fairly Standard Stuff and should cost less than $90.

Understand that in most X-braced guitars the bracing is asymmetrical and that right-handed guitars are braced to have the bass strings on the left side of the top. There shouldn't be any real mechanical problem with this; it's more a matter of tonal balance. Unless you have a highly developed ear, you probably won't hear the difference.

—*Rick Turner*

NECK RELIEF

The next step is to check the neck relief. If you push a string down at the first and 14th frets, you should see a bit of daylight between the bottom of the string and the seventh fret. This gap is known as the *relief,* and the correct amount of relief depends on how hard you play. The range is generally between .010 inches (the thickness of a common electric guitar high E string) and .026 inches (the thickness of a standard light-gauge G string on an acoustic).

On many older acoustics, particularly Martins, the neck relief is not adjustable. Most modern steel-string acoustics have an adjustable truss rod, which puts pressure or compression on the neck to counter the string tension. You can access the adjustment nut either at the peghead end (Gibsons and Yamahas, for example) or through the soundhole (most others). You can learn to adjust your own truss rods, but be *very* careful; it's easy to overdo it. Generally, a clockwise turn will flatten the relief and a counterclockwise turn will deepen the relief, but there's bound to be an acoustic guitar builder out there who doesn't follow this convention, damn his soul! I often make the more drastic rod adjustments over a period of

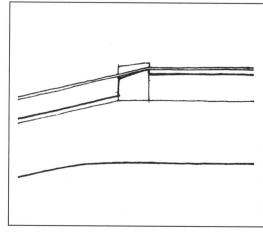

The nut's string slot should match the break angle of the string.

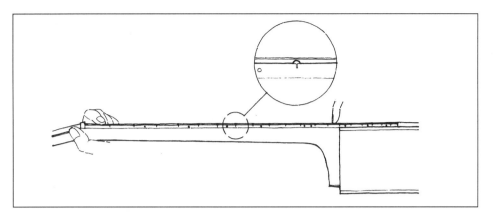

Check the neck relief by pushing down each string at the first and 14th frets and sighting the gap between the bottom of the string and the seventh fret.

several days, because the response is often a bit delayed, especially if the neck has been severely warped.

SADDLE ADJUSTMENTS

The next step in a typical setup is adjusting the action at the bridge saddle. On modern acoustics, the saddle is usually press-fit into a closed end slot, making it easy to simply pull out the saddle for action adjustments. If the action needs to be lower, I sand or file a bit off the bottom of the saddle and refit it in the slot. If the action needs to come up, I add a bone or wood veneer to the bottom of the saddle, file it to fit, and reinstall it in the slot. In either case, I also smooth the top surface of the saddle to eliminate any burrs, round it so it doesn't stress the strings too much, and polish it up.

On older guitars, the saddle is often glued into a longer, open-ended slot, making adjustments more time-consuming (and thus more expensive for you). On these guitars, I lower the action by filing, sanding, and polishing the saddle in place, while being careful not to damage or mar the guitar's bridge or top. Raising the action on these guitars usually means removing the old saddle and replacing it with a higher one.

For intonation-sensitive players, I often intonate the saddle to match the harmonics and fretted notes at the 12th fret. This procedure results in a zigzag line of string witness points, which compensates for the harmonic inaccuracies of differing string stiffnesses.

GET SET

So, how often should you bring your guitar in for a setup? I'd say at least once a year if you play a lot. It's a lot easier to set up a guitar that gets regular attention than to do one that only sees the top of a luthier's bench once every ten years. Also, your luthier can keep an eye on other aspects of your guitar's health, such as cracks, loose parts, fret wear, and neck angle.

Expect to pay between $35 and $75 for a setup. The exact price will depend on how much work is necessary to get your instrument into top form. Prices vary somewhat around the country. They're generally higher in urban areas like New York

---

COMPENSATING SADDLES

Q *How do compensating saddles and adjustable bridges affect a guitar's intonation?*

A Compensating saddles adjust for the fact that real-world strings do not stay in tune with mathematically derived fret positions, and the degree of "out-of-tuneness" changes depending on string stiffness and composition. This is why the usual compensation for acoustic guitars is a zigzag line with the low E (the stiffest string) having the longest length, the G being the shortest of the wound strings, and the B zigging back for a little more length than the G.

A fixed compensation, filed into your saddle, usually works fine as long as you stick with the same string action height, string gauge, and string brand. The Grandaddy, made by GVM, is one adjustable into-nation saddle available for acoustic guitars. Compensated saddles will probably change the sound of your guitar somewhat, however, so I wouldn't recommend using them without careful consideration, especially if you have a collectible guitar. For some musicians, being in tune is well worth any trade-off in tone or vintage value. Other musicians can make do with just about anything and sound in tune.

—Rick Turner

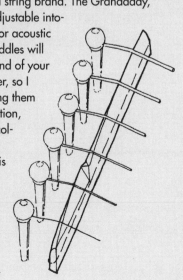

and Los Angeles, where it just costs more to run a business. Beware of cut-rate guitar repair; some inexperienced guitar-repair wannabes will cut prices just to gain clients and experience. While a setup is not major surgery, a good repair person will do a better job in less time than someone who is just learning.

You change the oil in your car every 3,000 miles, don't you? Well, your guitar deserves no less care, and you deserve a guitar that plays as well as you do. Take it in for a setup and enjoy your instrument at its peak performance.

CUTTING STRING SLOTS

Q *How deep should the string slots be cut into the nut?*

A String height over the fingerboard at the nut should be no higher and no lower then the height of the crown of the first fret. Cutting the string into the nut much higher increases the likelihood of pitch distortion and hard action over the first several frets. Seating them much lower results in buzzing on top of the first fret.

But rules are sometimes meant to be broken. In fact, you can usually cut the high E string a whisker lower than the first fret crown without a problem. On the low E string it's just the opposite. Cut the nut so the low E string seats a whisker higher.

The reason for cutting the low E string higher in the nut is that most steel-string acoustic guitars have a strong fundamental soundbox resonance peak (called the main wood/air resonance) in that pitch region. When you pop the massive low E string, it kicks the soundbox with a significant jolt of kinetic energy at or close to the same frequency of its characteristic main resonance peak. The soundbox responds by resonating at that frequency in an unusually energetic way. The soundbox will then feed energy back into the string at that frequency, since the saddle at the bridge allows energy to pass in both directions.

Energy kicked back into the vibrating string this way causes its excursion to move beyond its "normal" boundaries. Thus, it is prudent to allow the bit of additional clearance. Clearly, other guitars with main resonance peaks placed elsewhere probably will not experience this problem: i.e., small steel-strings and classic guitars have resonance peaks more often at A and correspondingly don't require any extra height at the nut.

—*William R. Cumpiano*

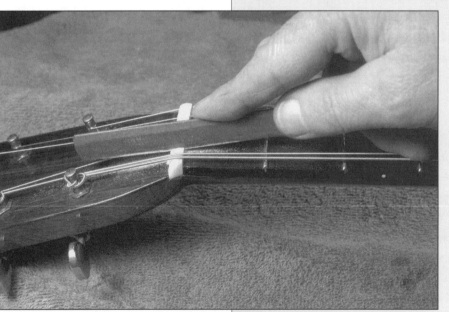

Setting the Action

Harry Fleishman

Any useful discussion of acoustic guitar setup should include a close look at the truss rod, the nut, and the saddle. Each of these parts contributes significantly to the way your guitar plays, and each can develop its own set of problems. You can make many of the adjustments I'll describe yourself if you're careful and use a little common sense. If you have a serious problem with your guitar, however, you should not hesitate to take it to a reputable luthier.

The action, or string height above the fretboard, is one of the first things to check when your guitar isn't playing quite right. Many musicians mistakenly use the truss rod to adjust the action; they tighten it, thinking that by arching the neck back they will lower the strings toward the fingerboard. A tightened truss rod *will* lower the action, but it often leads to a neck that buzzes severely. The misguided home repair guy then starts filing away at his frets until the neck is a basket case.

The truss rod's job is to straighten the neck and compensate for the upward pull of the strings. It should not be used to adjust the action of the neck. If the action is too high at the nut, it is the nut that needs adjustment. If the action is too high in the middle and upper positions, it is usually the saddle that needs to be lowered. Let's take a look at the truss rod first. Once it is properly adjusted, we can move on to the nut and the saddle.

THE TRUSS ROD

Adjusting the neck using the truss rod is a delicate operation. If it is necessary to tighten your truss rod, I recommend setting aside plenty of time to do it. When I build a guitar for a musician, I custom-design the neck to meet his or her playing style and to accommodate a variety of string gauges. Changing to a heavier string may require a slight tightening of the rod. A lighter string may need a little backing off of the rod. Occasionally a small adjustment can be made, and the guitar will be ready to play immediately. Often, however, the neck will need time to get used to its new position.

Most factory guitars, including Taylors, newer Martins, and Guilds, use truss rods that are tightened with a clockwise turn. That is, rotating the rod clockwise brings the strings closer to the fretboard. Occasionally with double-action rods (rods that adjust in both directions), a clockwise turn may actually raise the strings. If the neck has not been damaged by heat or a long-neglected warp, a little rotation should cause the desired effect. If your neck is badly warped, get professional help.

On many guitars, the truss rod can be accessed via the headstock. For others (including the guitars I build), you need to reach into the soundhole. When the rod access is inside the soundhole, special care, and probably special tools, may be needed. Take a deep breath, count to ten, and if you're sure you want to do your own adjustment, go for it. I like to make neck adjustments with the strings under normal tension; it lets me see the real effect on the neck. I assume that most of you do not have a fully equipped shop with guitar-holding fixtures. Therefore, I suggest asking a friend to help by holding the guitar steady. First, mark the rod's nut with a felt pen so you can return it to its starting

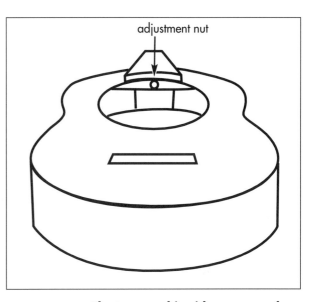

The truss rod is either accessed via the soundhole (above) or the headstock (below).

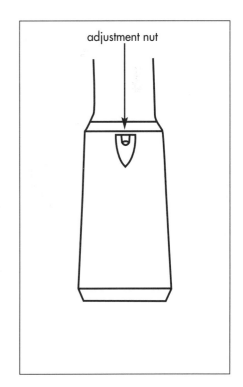

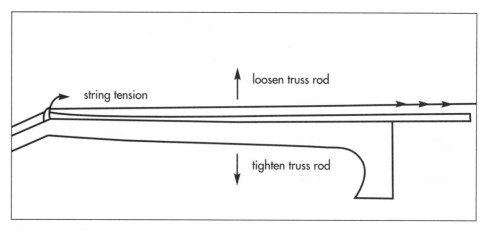

Tightening the truss rod compensates for the upward pull of the strings, and loosening it allows the neck to bow.

point. Then, slightly loosen the rod and see that it turns freely. If it is bound or frozen, do not try to adjust it further unless you have a great deal of experience or a deep-seated wish to break the rod and replace the neck. If it moves smoothly, put a bit of lubricant on the threads and work it in around the nut. I use a toothpick or a bit of old guitar string for this job. Then put the truss rod nut back to where it was when you started, using the mark you made as a reference.

Now is a good time to ask your friend to hold the guitar and press down gently on the nut, making the truss rod's work easier. Gently give the truss rod about a one-quarter turn. Now fret the guitar at the first and last frets and use the string as a straight-edge to see if the neck is getting flatter. The rod's effect is usually most apparent between the fifth and seventh frets. I like to see a little light between the string and the fret in the middle of the neck. If it looks right, wait a few minutes and recheck. If it seems to need more tightening, be very careful. If your rod is working correctly, you shouldn't have to crank it hard to get good results.

If you are getting areas of buzz in an otherwise well-adjusted neck, you may need a fret job. Fret work is a very fussy job, demanding accuracy to less than a thousandth of an inch. It also requires specialized tools. Contact a reputable luthier to do your fret work.

THE NUT

Often, guitarists adjust their truss rods when what really needs work is either the nut or the bridge. If the first few frets feel stiff and hard to play, the nut probably needs work. A nut that is not cut deeply enough will make chords in the first few positions difficult to play. A nut that is too deep will buzz like a sitar. If the strings are hard to tune, again the nut may be to blame. Although it can be tricky to make a nut play well, if you are careful and take your time, you can probably improve the playability of your nut. You will need a few unusual tools for this job, so unless you want to make a small investment, go to a luthier.

Very fine, small files allow you to make the grooves for the strings with great precision. It is the careful fitting of these grooves that makes the nut play well and sound clean. Nut files come in many sizes to match the diameters of guitar strings. You don't need all of them. You can make each file do the duty of many by rocking the file slightly as you work. Pay special attention to the shape of the groove. The object is to end up with a groove that neither binds the string nor causes it to buzz. If you file too deeply, you can fill in the groove with a little superglue and start over. Be careful, wear eye protection, and don't overdo it. Place one tiny drop in the groove and sprinkle a bit of baking soda

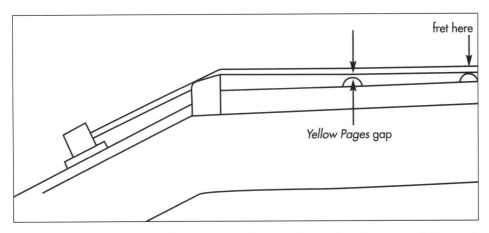

If your nut is the right height, you should be able to fret the second fret and just fit a scrap of paper from the *Yellow Pages* between the first fret and the string.

over it as the glue sets. This will harden into a very good simulation of bone, letting you regroove the nut as if you had not messed up. Only you and I will know. Gently file until a scrap of paper from the *Yellow Pages* will slip in between the first fret and the string when fretted at the second fret (see illustration).

Even a well-fitted nut can bind and mess up your ability to tune. One evening I received a phone call from Scott Bennett, who had been touring the world and recording for 20 years on a guitar I made him. He was backstage at the Boulder Theater waiting to go on, and the D string on his guitar was binding and making a little squeaking noise whenever he tuned it. You've probably had the same problem. I immediately drove across town to fix his nut. After a moment's diagnosis I took out a no. 2 pencil and put a little graphite under each string in the groove of his nut. The problem was solved. If you don't overdo it, you'll find that a bit of graphite (pencil lead isn't really lead, you know) can work wonders to stop strings from binding.

THE SADDLE

If your action still feels wrong and the neck has been properly adjusted, it is time to look at the saddle. Lowering the action may require removing a bit of material from the saddle. Raising it may mean a new saddle or a shim under your existing saddle. If some strings are fine and others are too high or low, you should consider recontouring the top of your saddle. Otherwise, it is simpler and safer to make adjustments to the bottom. To raise the action, I recommend using a new, properly fitted saddle, preferably made of bone— although many new synthetics are available. It is not always practical to have a new saddle made or to make one yourself. If you can't get one, I suggest shimming what you have. Hardwood veneers are a good choice and readily available. Veneers are commonly .032-inch thick. They can be sanded if you need a thinner shim or stacked to achieve a taller one. At least half of the saddle should be within the bridge slot or it may tip forward or even break the leading edge of the bridge. Be extra careful if you have an under-saddle pickup. Changing your saddle could affect the string-to-string balance.

If you need to lower the height of your saddle, sandpaper attached to a flat surface works well. Simply slide the saddle back and forth across the abrasive, being careful to keep the bottom of the saddle flat. It helps to mark with a pencil how much material you wish to remove and then sand to that mark.

Setting up your own guitar can be very satisfying. You will be most successful if you work when you are not in a hurry and if you take extra care at each step. Good luck.

Saddle and Bridge Pin Materials

Marshall Newman

Custom bridge pins of bone, ebony, and fossilized ivory from Fossil Ivory King.

In guitars as well as in life, little things count for a lot. Today's flattop guitar players face a wealth of choices in pursuit of the perfect acoustic sound: dozens of manufacturers and individual guitar makers, a variety of sizes and body shapes, a wide range of available tonewoods, and scores of string options. With so much to consider, saddles and bridge pins receive scant attention. They deserve more.

One look at the basic acoustic guitar design shows why the saddle is so important. The guitar's strings vibrate along the length of the scale, and the saddle transmits those vibrations to the soundboard, where much of the sound develops. Bridge pins help anchor the strings to the bridge, usually by holding the ball ends of the strings under the bridge plate (the reinforcing piece of wood directly under the bridge inside the soundboard). Since this anchor point is removed from the vibrating portion of the strings (separated by the bridge and saddle), the pins do not transmit string vibrations. They affect the guitar's tone by changing the mass and vibration potential of the bridge. The soundboard, bridge, bridge plate, bracing, and body all play roles in shaping the instrument's sound, but the saddle provides a great deal of the source signal and concurrently filters the string vibrations, limiting or eliminating certain tones as a result of the material from which it is made.

SADDLE UP

Fifty years ago, the saddle material of choice was elephant ivory, with ebony a distant second. Hard, easy to work, and beautiful, ivory offered clear, smooth tonal response. However, rising prices and the slaughter of elephants for their ivory (which eventually led to the international embargo on elephant ivory) caused Gibson to turn to wood, plastic, ceramic, and even adjustable metal saddles on many models by the 1960s. Martin switched to plastic saddles in 1973 and two years later changed to Micarta, the high-pressure laminate it continues to use today.

Many guitarists accustomed to the rich, full tone that ivory imparts were unimpressed. To their ears, these early ivory substitutes simply didn't work as well as the real thing. Bone emerged in the 1970s as a natural substitute saddle material. Similar to ivory but even harder, and readily available, bone's only drawback was some inconsistency in density. Two other natural substitutes became available in the early 1990s: mammoth ivory and fossilized walrus ivory, both harvested at construction sites and along streambeds and ocean cliffs in Alaska. Color (usually darker than ivory or bone), density (mammoth ivory is sometimes rather soft), and cost (several times that of bone) have been the main drawbacks of these materials, but each has its partisans.

The 1990s also saw the introduction of a new generation of synthetic saddle materials. Tusq, created by Graph Tech Guitar Labs, is an artificial ivory molded under extreme heat and pressure. Hard and easy to shape, Tusq saddles are used by several manufacturers, including Taylor, Larrivée, and Breedlove. The Cleartone saddle from Fishman Transducers combines a hard yet resilient proprietary material called Fishbone with a unique five-key-hole design that enables the base of the saddle to seat evenly and firmly in the saddle slot and gives each string a separate vibration path to the bridge and soundboard.

California guitar tech Larry Cragg, who cares for instruments owned by such rock stars as Neil Young, put three saddle materials to the test. He set up a Taylor 514-C—a grand auditorium guitar with mahogany back and sides and a cedar top—with a Cleartone saddle, a Tusq saddle, and a bone saddle; used the same brand of light-gauge phosphor-bronze strings in each trial; and recorded his impressions.

"Tusq showed lots of power, especially on the lower strings," he said, "but with some blending of individual string tones and a bit of edginess at the top end. The Cleartone saddle showed good separation and clarity—the design really works—but wasn't as rich tonewise. Bone—a nice, dense piece—didn't have the highs of Tusq or the Cleartone saddle and lacked string separation at the bottom and top, but it was the richest and most 'natural' sounding of the three."

Luthier Al Milburn, who does a range of repairs at his shop in Kensington, California, also investigated the differences between bone and mammoth ivory saddles. "Of the two, bone has fuller and crisper tone with more dynamic range," he said. "Mammoth ivory has a softer, woodier sound and isn't quite as bright. A fingerstyle player would likely appreciate the sparkling tone of bone. A bluegrass flatpicker, whose role is often rhythm accompaniment, probably would prefer the warmth of mammoth ivory."

A Tusq nut: artificial ivory molded under extreme heat and pressure.

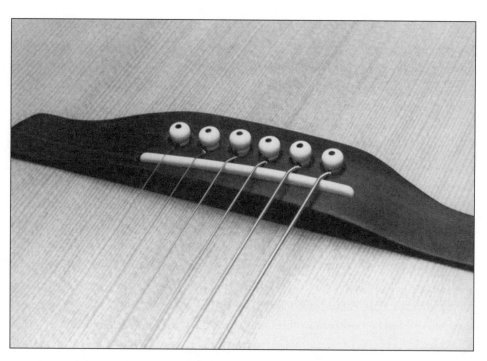

Tusq saddles are used by several large-scale guitar manufacturers.

Fingerstyle guitarist and guitar maker Eric Schoenberg has one overriding requirement when it comes to choosing material for saddles. "It has to be hard. A good, hard saddle works best." He has used fossilized walrus ivory on several instruments and likes the results. "Fossilized walrus ivory is really hard stuff, with a nice, crisp sound," he said. "I don't hear much difference between it and elephant ivory."

BRIDGE PINS

Fifty years ago, bridge pins were made of Bakelite plastic or ebony. Over 40 years or so, various types of plastic pins came into use. Then, in the 1990s, in an apparent backlash against the aesthetics of plastic, bridge pins became available in a range of natural and natural-looking materials, including boxwood, mammoth ivory, brass, fossilized walrus ivory, bone, water buffalo horn, and ivoroid.

Larry Cragg has tried all of these materials at one time or another, and he voiced some strong opinions. "Plastic is light and easy to drive, but it seems to absorb a lot of the highs and lows. Brass adds plenty of sustain but isn't very loud. Mammoth ivory offers good highs and good sustain. I really like ebony pins, because they add fullness, especially to the low end. But my favorite bridge pin setup is ebony on the three low strings and water buffalo horn on the three high strings. The water buffalo horn is light and hard, and it really brings out the highs."

Al Milburn took a more cautious view. "Tone is pretty subjective," he said, "and while it's difficult to predict the tone that particular bridge pins will impart, the difference will be subtle. The important thing is that the pins fit snugly in the bridge and seat the ball end of the strings firmly against the bridge plate."

If you're interested in changing your saddle or bridge pins to see how different materials affect your guitar's sound, you'll find the cost reasonable. Prices vary, but an experienced luthier usually can make and install a new compensated saddle for less than $100. Bridge pins are similarly affordable; you could replace your plastic bridge pins with ebony for as little as $15 (or you could splurge for a set of mammoth ivory or fossilized walrus ivory pins for as much as $120). While most warranties are not affected by saddle changes made by authorized repair technicians, it's always a good idea to check before having any work done. So go ahead, take a moment to focus on a few of the guitar's many details. You may be surprised by the results.

Fret Maintenance

Rick Turner

This protruding fret is also loose and lifting off the fingerboard.

Next to setups, the most common job in a guitar repair shop is leveling frets, also known as a grind and polish or a mill, crown, and polish. The terms refer to basically resurfacing the tops of the frets. The job involves leveling the tops of the frets, recrowning to restore the rounded tops, and then bringing the frets up to a scratch-free polish so the strings will not scrape if you bend notes. Well-cared-for frets can make all the difference between the guitar from heaven and the guitar from hell.

The cost for fret work and all guitar repair varies around the country. In Los Angeles, the current hourly rate for a luthier's time is around $45 to $55. It's less in the middle of the country and much more in New York. Prices for fret work vary based on how much material needs to be removed, how large the fret wire is (larger takes longer), and just how perfectly you need the guitar to play above the neck joint.

FRET WIRE

Most fret wire is made of a metal alloy known as nickel silver or German silver. There is no true silver in this material, which is a nonferrous (nonmagnetic) alloy of nickel and copper; the word *silver* refers to its color. Nickel silver has been used for many years as

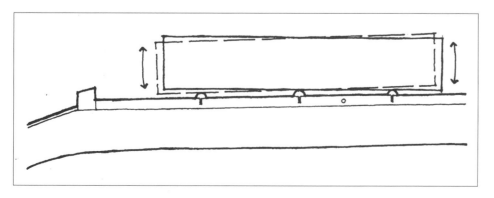

When leveling fret tops, luthiers check for undue rocking with a straightedge, with each fret acting as a pivot.

a silver substitute in jewelry and as the metal of choice for optical instruments, eyeglass frames, clock parts, and even some metal-bodied National guitars. It tarnishes slowly, machines and forms easily, and wears quite well. Brass fret wire is sometimes seen on cheap instruments, but it wears poorly and tarnishes more readily than nickel silver.

In the 1800s many guitars were built with bar fret wire, which is basically rectangular in cross section. Bar frets were nicked on the bottom with a miniature sharp hatchet to create barbs to help anchor them, and they were installed in slots the full width of the wire. C.F. Martin still provides two styles of bar fret wire for restorers of antique instruments.

Modern fret wire, which is shaped like a round-topped T in cross section, is made by running nickel silver wire through a series of rollers with grooves that form the crown, the tang, and the barbs on the tang, which help hold the frets into the slotted fingerboard. Fret wire is available in a dizzying range of sizes, but the most important dimensions to a player are the crown height and width. Acoustic players are most familiar with what is now in the "medium" range of fret wire size. Very small fret wire is generally reserved for mandolins and banjos, while jumbo and super-jumbo is often used on electric guitars and basses. I have noticed a trend toward the use of larger fret wire on both classical guitars and electric guitarists' acoustics. There is some feeling that the larger wire increases attack and sustain by putting more mass at the string end; large fret wire also makes vibrato techniques easier in both blues and classical styles.

The most important aspects of fret work are the evenness of fret height, fret top shape, and fret top polish. The fret tops must be absolutely even in height relative to the bottom of the strings. You should see an overall forward bow in the neck, which is reflected in the fret tops. There can be minor hills and dales of a few thousandths of an inch in the fingerboard surface itself (though it's not ideal), but there should be no fret tops higher or lower than their immediate neighbors. High or low frets will cause localized buzzing.

PROTRUDING FRETS

Q *What can I do about protruding or lifting fret edges?*

A Protruding frets are a common problem, even on high-quality guitars, and especially those with ebony fingerboards. It can take years for ebony to stabilize completely, and even then, if the guitar is moved to a drier climate, the ebony fingerboard will shrink somewhat. The problem is less pronounced with rosewood fingerboards. The fret wire, being metal, is unaffected by humidity changes, and when the wood shrinks, the fret ends protrude. This movement can also break any glue bond in the fret slot, and because frets are usually hammered in under tension, when the glue breaks, the fret end can pop up, even though there are barbs on the fret tang.

For a guitar repair whiz, this is no big deal to fix. Squeeze in a little superglue, press the fret ends down, file the fret ends, and level, crown, and polish the frets. End of problem, at least until next time. I like to use lemon oil on fingerboard surfaces; it looks and feels good and seems to keep ebony and rosewood more stable by preventing overdrying of the wood surface.

—*Rick Turner*

LEVELING

How do you know if you need a fret level? You need a luthier's touch if you have noticeable divots or grooves in the frets under notes you play often (luthiers can tell a lot about what kind of music you play just by reading the fret wear), if there is a particular spot on the neck where you get fret buzz, or if your fret tops are very flattened out, which can cause intonation to go sharp. Many players just get used to guitars that are in need of fret work; the deterioration takes place over time and is not a matter of good one day, bad the next. But it's like not changing the oil or not rotating the tires on your car—the net result is poor performance.

There are almost as many ways to level frets as there are luthiers; everyone comes up with his or her specific set of procedures. Whether one uses a stone, a file, or sandpaper to level frets, and a triangular file or a concave diamond file to round frets off, is of little consequence. Ultimately it's the results that count. Here are the steps your guitar would go through if it wound up on a bench in my shop.

The first step is reading the neck and fingerboard, looking for evenness of string relief, and checking bass and treble sides of the fingerboard. We need to determine if there are any oddities in the way the neck bows when string tension is up full. There are a surprising number of guitar necks out there that look fine with no strings and then go wacko when they're strung up. So when we level the frets, we may want to file in a little extra space here or there to compensate for slight kinks that are only evident under string tension. There are several techniques for dealing with under-tension neck bumps. Master luthier Dan Erlewine has designed a jig to hold stringless guitars in a simulation of their strung-up condition. Some clamp the neck in a cradle and put weights on the guitar to bow the neck, and others just work from memory on the problem areas.

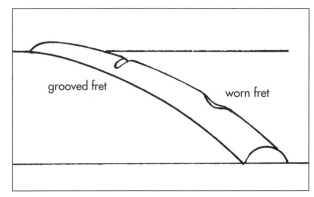

This fret is worn to the point where it needs milling or replacement.

The next step is the actual leveling of the tops of the frets. Some use long flat files, some use oilstones, and I often use a piece of quarter-inch plate glass with a handle onto which I stick some emery paper or 220 sandpaper. By sanding or grinding lengthwise up and down the fingerboard, I make the tops of the frets true to one another, much like planing a board to get it perfectly straight. I constantly check my progress with a set of precision straightedges, looking for any undue rocking with each fret acting as a pivot. By using several different lengths of straightedge, I can check the overall relationship of fret tops and zoom in to check shorter sections of the neck. The challenge is getting the fret tops true without removing any more fret material than absolutely necessary.

With acoustic guitar fingerboards, the biggest problem area is right at the neck-to-body joint. That is a virtual hinge point, so it often has a hump or dip. To make matters worse, the geometry of the fingerboard is subject to climatic changes. Humidity can cause the top to rise and fall, and it takes the fingerboard extension with it. Sometimes luthiers just have to ask if playing high up the neck is really necessary for your style. If not, they might not worry too much about perfectly level frets all the way to the soundhole. If you do need it perfect all the way up, your guitar may need to be refretted.

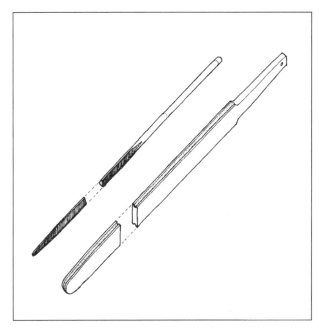

Some luthiers use a triangular steel file (left) to recrown fret tops, but I prefer Stewart-MacDonald's concave diamond file (right).

It is not uncommon for a fret to come loose and pop up just enough to cause problems. As the luthier is leveling, the offending fret is pressed down even with its neighbors; once the leveling block or file is off, however, the fret pops up a few thousandths of an inch, causing a buzz. I find that loose frets sound different as the leveling file or sanding block passes over them, giving me a clue that there is a problem. The fix is to glue down the fret end(s) or center(s) with superglue and move on, or in severe cases to recurve and/or replace the fret(s).

A note of caution: although excess superglue can be cleaned off many polyester and urethane finishes with solvent, superglue bonds mightily with nitrocellulose lacquer, and superglue remover is a great lacquer stripper. So, if you go near your guitar with superglue for any reason, be very careful. Building up your nails with superglue? Don't do it near your instrument.

CROWNING

After leveling, I recrown the fret tops as close to their original shape as possible. My favorite tool for this is the Erlewine-designed concave diamond file set available from

Stewart-MacDonald Guitar Shop Supply. Many luthiers use similar steel files, and some use triangular files with the corners ground safe so as not to leave scratches on the fingerboard. For production work, I use a diamond fret crowning file in a reciprocating air-powered filer that makes short work of the crowning operation, but for most repair work, I just do it the old-fashioned way—by hand.

After a first run-through at recrowning, I will once again check the neck with the straightedges, and if it seems OK I'll string the guitar up to make sure there are no high frets causing buzzes. This is the time to make sure that no frets were ground too low in the recrowning step. At this point, the frets look like hell, but the guitar should play cleanly.

POLISHING

After recrowning, the fret tops need to be brought up to a fine polish. I go through successive steps of carbide grit sand paper—320, 400, and 600—then successive grits of 3M Scotchbrite—red, gray, and white. With the gray and white Scotchbrite, I'll use a little lemon oil and work first parallel to the frets and then lengthwise over the fingerboard. For the final touch, I'll polish the frets with either microfine sandpaper—in the 3200-grit region—or with some liquid buffing compound on a cloth wrapped around a hard foam pad.

When you get your guitar back, there should be no obvious cross-grain scratches in the fingerboard (in the direction of the fret wire). Your fingerboard should look better than new, as long as it didn't have any divots or dings to start with.

If you play with a heavy touch, you should know that even the best luthiers cannot make a fingerboard absolutely buzz free. There will come a point when you can hit the strings hard enough to make them buzz on any guitar. Players are often unaware of just how hard they play, and many guitarists are a bit rough around the edges with their right-hand technique. The very best you can hope for is that the instrument will play with absolute consistency at any given dynamic level.

How many times can a fretboard be milled, crowned, and polished before you need a refret? There are a lot of factors at work here. Let's assume that there are no bad humps or dips in the board, so all you're dealing with is the basic job as described. If you don't wait until the divots in your frets are really bad, your guitar should withstand three or four fret jobs before you just don't have enough fret height left.

FRET LINGO

BARB A small bump on the fret tang that helps lock it into the fret slot.

BEAD The round upper portion of the fret.

CROWN The shape of the top of the fret bead.

TANG A breakfast drink. Also, the lower portion of the fret that fits into the slot in the fingerboard.

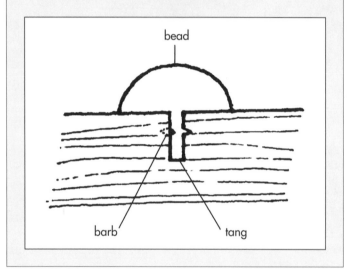

Refretting

Rick Turner

Just as there comes a time when merely rotating the tires on your car won't do and you need to buy new ones, so too comes a time when a mill, crown, and polish just isn't enough and you need to replace the frets on your guitar. There are several conditions that indicate that a refret may be needed: frets that are too worn-out to be brought back to playing condition by a fret mill; a hump in the guitar's neck that can only be fixed by planing and sanding the fingerboard; and a guitar that needs a neck reset, a job that often works best when accompanied by a refret.

Under any conditions calling for a refret, you can be assured that this is fairly routine work for a competent repairer. A proper refret can be virtually undetectable, and in many cases it is an opportunity to greatly improve the guitar's playability. As for the effect on your guitar's resale value, that is a matter for the vintage dealers to obsess over. Collectors who balk at having a guitar refretted "because it will hurt the guitar's value" should consider whether they love guitars as instruments or whether perhaps they should be collecting Picassos instead.

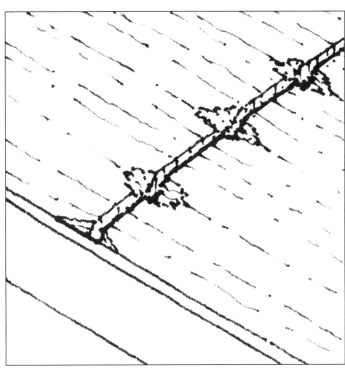

If an old fret isn't removed carefully, it can chip the slot.

CHOOSING FRET WIRE

Once you have decided that your instrument needs a refret, it is time to think about fret wire size. There is a dizzying array of possibilities, and there may be valid reasons to consider going to a different size than what you are used to. For instance, I have been seeing more use of jumbo fret wire on classical guitars recently; the feeling is that the greater mass of the jumbo wire gives better attack and sustain to the notes. Players used to electric guitars may also be more comfortable with larger fret wire than is normal on acoustics. Beware, though, and don't be talked into a nonstandard fret wire based on some fad. You should be willing to consider new options, but you should also be sure you have a good reason for change.

A case in point is Robben Ford, who once asked me to refret his Strat with jumbo fret wire. He was experiencing severe tendinitis because he was clamping down too hard on the frets with the fingers of his left hand. His theory was that the larger fret wire (I used Dunlop 6100) would cause him to lighten up his left-hand touch to keep the notes from going sharp. And he was right: he loved the large fret wire, and it solved his problem.

Before starting a refret, the luthier should get a read on the fingerboard with strings at normal tension. I use a set of precision straightedges and sight the neck to find any weird spots that might need special care when prepping the fingerboard. You cannot read the neck by sighting down the sides of the fingerboard, because worn fingerboard edges can be very deceiving. I've worked on many guitars that looked much worse than they actually were.

REMOVING THE OLD FRETS

The first step of a refret is cleanly removing the old frets. If this isn't done carefully, the fret barbs can pull up chips of fingerboard wood on either side of the fret slots (see illustration, page 69). The trick is to heat each fret prior to pulling it out. Many repairers use a soldering iron, but I use an American Beauty resistance soldering station with a pair of electrodes to run a low voltage at high current through each fret. The current puts the heat right at the fret slot, thus causing the fret to heat up evenly, and breaks loose any glue that might have been used to help anchor the fret into the fingerboard. This process also seems to help temporarily plasticize the wood, so that when the frets are removed (I pull them out with modified end nippers), there is a minimum of chipping. This defretting technique has been a lifesaver with vintage instruments and instruments with superglued or epoxied frets. One caveat: take care around celluloid bindings; they are flammable!

PREPPING THE FINGERBOARD

The next procedure is prepping the fingerboard by sanding with flat or radiused blocks to straighten and smooth the surface. This step can involve several judgment calls. Do you sand out all of the fingernail divots? Do you sand a lot of fingerboard to straighten out the neck? Are the inlays going to need removal and replacement? How are you going to deal with fingerboard problems over the body? Too much sanding of the fingerboard can alter the feel of the neck, and it is easy to accidentally sand through inlays.

I have come to prefer the least possible sanding of the fingerboard surface. Usually even deep divots won't affect the refretability or the playability of the neck, and if they are really bothersome, they can be filled with superglue and leveled off. I'd much rather remove and/or replace an inlay than try to save it at the expense of playability. And sometimes you do have to get radical at the end of the fingerboard that's glued to the guitar's top. On one of his guitars, Jackson Browne simply had the frets removed from the body end of the fingerboard because there was such a rise in that area. He figured that since he didn't play that guitar up there, it just didn't matter. On other guitars where the fingerboard takes a dive over the body, it may be best to loosen the fingerboard and insert a tapered shim to level the playing surface. Sometimes it is better to replace an entire fingerboard to get the desired results, rather than jumping through hoops to restore one that will never play right anyway.

With bound fingerboards there is a question of whether to lay the fret ends over the binding in the Martin fashion or to allow the binding to cap the fret ends as is common with Gibsons (see illustrations, page 71). Here again we run into the collector-versus-player controversy. If you refret a Gibson in the Martin style, the guitar will probably feel better, and you can widen the spacing of the strings at the nut if you want to. I find that on many Gibsons, the nubs of binding at the end of the frets are annoying or even downright dangerous, and I usually file them down even on guitars that aren't being refretted. And while refretting bound fretboards with overlaid fret ends costs more than doing an

---

WORN FINGERBOARDS

 Can you recommend a material to fill the worn spots in my fingerboard?

A Assuming that the neck has not been refretted several times (thereby diminishing the thickness of the fingerboard), the frets can be removed and the fingerboard can be surfaced smooth and refretted. If the ruts are too deep, they can be filled using a mixture of sawdust and glue or just plain superglue, though this will no doubt show up, especially on a rosewood fingerboard. (Ebony is more forgiving.) If neither of the first two options is acceptable, and if any vintage consideration can be outweighed, then the old fingerboard can be removed and a new one put on. Refretting will probably be necessary in all three scenarios, since play that produces such wear on the fingerboard will most likely have destroyed the frets as well.

—*Dick Boak*

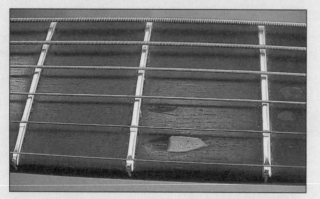

The divot in this fingerboard is so deep that it needed to be filled (and now needs refilling).

unbound board, trying to refret a Gibson in a way that makes it look original is even more expensive—it's like inlaying each and every fret. By the way, don't let anyone convince you that binding has to be removed in order to refret a guitar.

Along with leveling and sanding the fingerboard surface comes prepping the fret slots. If the guitar has been refretted before, the slots may be getting spongy or too wide to properly hold new frets. In such cases I will wick a bit of superglue into the end grain on either side of each slot. This restores the hardness and will make up a bit of the tolerance needed for the new fret tangs. In the case of any significant fingerboard sanding, the fret slots are likely to be too shallow. I use a Dremel mini-router with a very fine tapered dental burr to deepen the slots; this works well on bound or unbound fingerboards. Fine-bladed saws also work just fine on unbound fingerboards, but use caution when working over the body. You don't want fret slots in the top of your guitar!

INSTALLING THE NEW FRETS

There are several common methods for putting frets into the prepped fingerboard. The traditional method is to slightly overarch each piece of fret wire and tap the fret down into the slot with a light hammer, working carefully from the ends toward the center of the fret. The trick is to not overhammer any one spot along the length of the fret wire; this can make the fret spring back out of the fret slot. If there is to be any residual springiness in the fret, you want it helping to hold down the ends. Sometimes, if a fret keeps buzzing, you may need to glue it down.

Another method for inserting frets is using an arbor press with a curved shoe that matches the fingerboard radius. This is a commonly used technique in factories where conditions can be carefully controlled, but it is less often seen in guitar repair shops. It is a method best suited to bolt-on electric guitar necks where the guitar body does not get in the way when you move the neck through the press.

In the past few years, a number of luthiers have tried widening out the fret slots and bedding in the frets with epoxy. The theory is that this will allow the player to refret the fingerboard an infinite number of times, since the fret is not depending on the tightness of the wood to hold it in place. This practice has caused some controversy, though, because some say that the guitar's sound is compromised by not having a tight, direct connection between the frets and the fingerboard.

My own method generally involves lightly hammering in the frets and getting them as level as possible. Then I clamp the frets and fingerboard (neck, guitar, and all) into a specially made caul that contacts the ends and centers of all the frets, assuring that the fret tops are relatively level with one another. I then inject superglue into the ends of the fret slots just under the fret tangs. The glue wicks into the slots and up and around the tangs and barbs, totally locking the frets into place. Once the glue dries, I unclamp the whole thing, clean up any excess glue, and proceed with trimming the fret ends and dealing with any finish touch-up needed on the fingerboard edges.

At this point, it's back to the mill, crown, and polish, and then the job is complete. If the fingerboard prep and the fret installation were done carefully, the fret mill should involve a minimum of fret-height filing, and you will be playing for years before you need another refret.

A Martin-style bound fret end (top) and a Gibson-style capped fret end.

JUMBO FRETS

Q *What are the advantages and disadvantages of refretting with jumbo fret wire?*

A The installation of wide or jumbo frets on any instrument is a decision that must be based strictly on personal preference. The advisability of altering a vintage or collectible piece from original condition is a consideration, but fret installation is a process that is fairly easy to reverse. Wide frets can cause slight intonation problems, since the fulcrum point is less defined, but maintaining a correct crown as frets begin to flatten out from hard play can remedy this problem. Some players, especially electric guitarists who have gotten used to wider frets, will insist on refretting their acoustics, and there is nothing wrong with that. Players who are speculating about making the change without knowing exactly what they want should probably be encouraged to stick with what they have.

—Dick Boak

Caring for Your Guitar's Finish

Frank Ford

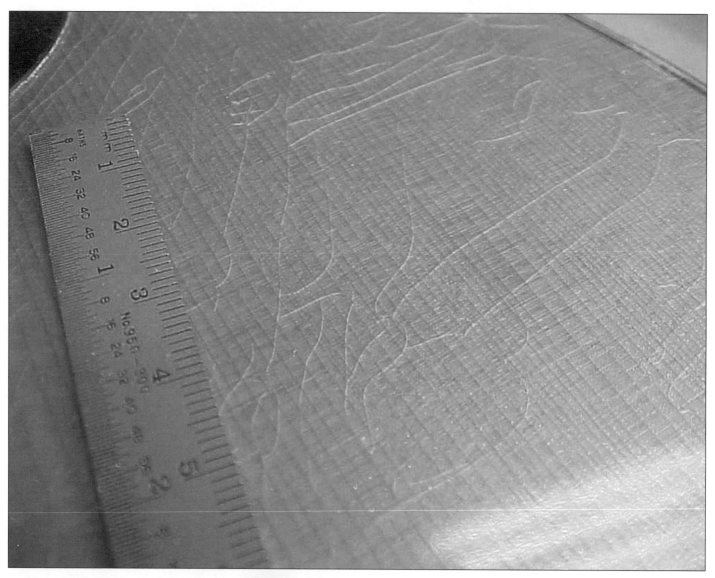

The classic "checked" lacquer finish.

Shiny or dull, colored or clear, the first thing you see when you look at a guitar is its finish. The finish may have a subtle effect on tone as it vibrates along with other parts of the instrument, but its real job is to keep the guitar looking good. It's a good idea to know a bit about your guitar's finish so you can better maintain it.

Historically, guitars have been finished with many different materials and techniques. Water-based finishes, penetrating oils, and natural, violin-type varnishes are rarely used on standard acoustic guitars. Nowadays, most guitars are finished with shellac, lacquer, or a catalyzed polymer. The finish may be highly glossy, completely dull and flat, or somewhere in between ("satin"). It may be clear or colored, transparent or opaque. It's tempting to think that a dull or satin finish is more natural or that a colored finish is heavy, but neither is necessarily true.

A high-gloss clear finish enhances wood grain because its reflective brilliance acts like a lens through which we view the guitar's surface. A glossy finish is easy to maintain; simply wipe the instrument with a soft cloth to keep it polished.

FRENCH POLISH

French polishing is an ancient technique used to apply a very thin high-gloss finish. It's a difficult skill to master and very labor intensive. The finisher applies coat after coat of shellac to build up the desired thickness, rubbing the surface with a shellac-soaked pad. To avoid getting the pad stuck in the fresh shellac surface when building the thickness of the finish, the luthier adds a bit of oil as a lubricant. The technique is very much like spit-shining a shoe. A French-polish finish may have a very level, high-gloss appearance similar to highly polished lacquer, or it may have a satin sheen that's slightly streaked in appearance when viewed in reflected light. Some luthiers, especially classical guitar makers, believe that French polish enhances the tone of a fine guitar. Today the technique is used most frequently on expensive classical guitars or on guitars made in places where spray equipment and solvents are at a premium, such as Paracho, Mexico.

Of all the conventional guitar finishes, French polish requires the most care. A natural resin dissolved in denatured alcohol, shellac has rather poor resistance to water, and it's usually applied in a very thin coating, so it offers very little resistance to scratches. The best way to care for it is to keep it clean and to avoid excessive handling. Abrasive guitar polishes are almost certain to cause premature wear. Natural shellac resin, which is amber-orange in color, is often used on dark woods. Sometimes, especially on Spanish classical guitars, orange shellac is used on the spruce top as well for a colored effect, but "bleached" or clear shellac is more frequently the choice on light-colored woods. For a deeper colored finish, the luthier may apply a stain or dye directly to the wood before French-polishing the instrument.

LACQUER

Between 1925 and 1930, guitar factories started using spray equipment to apply nitrocellulose lacquer, a fast-drying synthetic finish consisting of a resin dissolved in petroleum distillates. Like French-polish shellac, lacquer is an evaporative finish, meaning that the solvent simply evaporates, leaving the resin behind on the surface. Scratches can be touched up successfully because the lacquer can be dissolved or softened by its original solvent. An experienced finisher can blend and level new finish into an old scratch with surprisingly good results.

Lacquer saves a terrific amount of time compared to French polish. The finisher sprays successive coats of lacquer to build the finish to its final thickness, sanding the finish level between coats. Transparent or opaque coloring agents can be added to lacquer to provide a variety of effects. All the finish can be applied in just a few days, working for only a few minutes a day. After the last coat of lacquer has been allowed to dry for a week or more, the final polishing begins.

The luthier levels the finish by sanding with ultra-fine abrasives and buffs the guitar to a high gloss. Without the final sanding and buffing, the lacquer would be highly shiny and reflective, but the surface wouldn't be level. It would appear to have lumps, waves, or

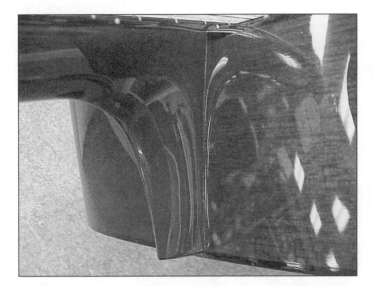
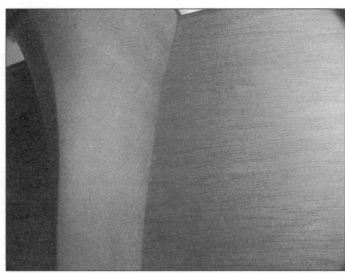

Two extremes: the glossiest finish versus the dullest.

"orange peel." It's the final leveling and buffing that gives lacquer its reputation for high-gloss elegance.

A lacquer finish is more durable than French polish, more resistant to scratches, body heat, and the normal wear of handling. Light scratches can be buffed out with power equipment, and the finish can be polished and maintained with a variety of finish care products and guitar polishes.

Lacquer does have a few undesirable properties, though. It has a nasty tendency to crack, craze, or check if exposed to sudden low temperatures. Most of us have seen instruments with these unsightly finish cracks. Lacquer also develops these cracks spontaneously if it's applied too thickly, and lacquer checks are nearly impossible to repair. Manufacturers may be tempted to apply thick layers of lacquer to cover small surface defects in the wood and to avoid rub-through in the process of leveling and polishing.

Certain players turn lacquer soft and sticky just by touching it. Unfortunately, the only solution to this particular problem is to refinish with a different material. Lacquer is sensitive to the vinyl covering on guitar stands as well as the vinyl backing of guitar straps and may soften and blister in areas of prolonged contact. Vinyl damage can usually be corrected by spot refinishing the affected area.

Some instruments are finished with a flat, low gloss, or satin lacquer. The dull or satin finish is precisely the same material as its glossy counterpart; it just has a chemical additive to make it dry less shiny. Satin or flat finishes are frequently used on less expensive models because they save labor, requiring no final leveling and polishing. Some manufacturers use a satin finish on the neck, and gloss on the body. The low-gloss finish is popular among performers because it doesn't reflect stage lighting. Lots of players simply prefer the look, too. One drawback to satin finish is that it tends to develop shiny patches where it's handled a lot, such as around the pickguard area and along the neck. It is usually impractical to try to correct this kind of wear. In general, low-gloss finishes are more difficult to restore or touch up as compared to high-gloss finishes.

CATALYZED POLYMERS

These days, the vast majority of acoustic guitars are not finished with either lacquer or French polish. Modern catalyzed polymer wood finishes have been developed to satisfy the factory's need for expedient production and the consumer's need for durability. These finishes are available in the same variety of colors and gloss as nitrocellulose lacquer. They're cured via a chemical reaction in which the liquid finish hardens to a solid material. The catalyst may be a second liquid added to the first, atmospheric moisture, or even ultraviolet light. Most catalyzed finishes are kinder to the atmosphere because they don't require as much solvent for application. Once the finish has cured, there's no solvent that will dissolve it. That means that a catalyzed finish is not likely to be damaged by any cleaning agent and won't react to contact with skin or vinyl. It can also be applied rather thickly without crazing, so it's ideal for inexpensive instruments where there might be surface imperfections to be filled.

Catalyzed finishes have gotten a bad rap because they have been associated with mass-produced inexpensive guitars. The good news is that these finishes can be applied sensitively in the same thickness as lacquer and can have virtually the same fine appearance and tonal properties. The bad news is that polymer finishes are not easily repaired. In order to do a really good finish touch-up, it is necessary to soften or dissolve the original finish. This is simply not possible with polymer finishes, so the best touch-ups will always be more visible, especially in reflected light.

How can you tell how your guitar was finished? It's best to ask the manufacturer, because it's virtually impossible to tell by looking at it. Your local guitar finish expert can test the finish with solvents to determine its composition and check its suitability for repair. Virtually all the Asian factories use catalyzed polymer finishes, as do many of the modern American producers, such as Taylor, Ovation, and Tacoma. Martin uses a catalyzed polymer finish on many of its lower-priced models. High-end Martins usually have lacquer on their bodies and catalyzed polymer finish on their necks. Gibson uses traditional nitrocellulose lacquer on all of its guitars.

Smaller factories and individual builders may also use catalyzed polymer, but the majority finish their guitars with lacquer. Santa Cruz, Collings, Goodall, and many other small shops pride themselves in their ability to achieve a nearly perfect polished surface with nitrocellulose lacquer. Just as French polishing all but disappeared in the '70s as lacquer became the standard finish, we are now seeing lacquer give way to modern catalyzed finishes. As long as vintage instruments are highly prized, however, builders and restorers will continue to practice "obsolete" finishing techniques.

Which finish is best? Clearly that's a matter of personal opinion. Luthiers and musicians are known for having strong opinions about guitars! Personally, I favor the modern catalyzed polymer finish because of its utility. It's so easy to live with and care for, and (properly applied) it's as beautiful as any.

LIFTING PICKGUARDS

Q *What type of glue should I use to reattach a lifting pickguard?*

A Pickguards tend to shrink over the years due to a slow loss of plasticizers (which keep them flexible). Pickguards are commonly made from cellulose nitrate—

celluloid—which is a notoriously unstable plastic. This virtual antique among plastics (developed in the 19th century) is still used by many manufacturers because it can be formulated into very convincing substitutes for elephant ivory and tortoiseshell. The process for making celluloid seems to be more art than science, and the stability varies from batch to batch. The shrinking of the pickguard, not the lifting, can pull the top strongly enough to crack it. There are a couple of approaches to fixing the problem, and neither involves just gluing the curled part down. The best solution is to completely remove the pickguard, thus relieving the stress on the top. Then you can either put on a self-stick pickguard or carefully restore the original. To do this, heat it in an oven at about 150 degrees Fahrenheit sandwiched between two pieces of plate glass. This relaxes the plastic, completes most of the shrinkage, and gets it flat again. Then glue it back on with 3M spray 90 contact adhesive, carefully masking the top around the area of the pickguard. The pickguard will be smaller than the original "footprint," so try to center it as best as you can and then touch up the finish around the reattached pickguard. It won't look factory fresh, but at least you'll preserve the original design. Many manufacturers are now attaching pickguards with an industrial grade of 3M double-stick tape, which is available from Stewart-MacDonald's Guitar Shop Supply.

—Rick Turner

Fixing Rattles

Frank Ford

It's a good idea to tighten the nuts on your guitar's tuners if you hear something rattling.

Your entire guitar vibrates when you play it: the top most of all, but even the neck and peghead are moved by the vibrating strings' energy. Any loose part on your guitar may buzz or rattle audibly, sometimes only when certain notes are played. Parts don't have to be visibly loose to rattle, and it can be quite a job to chase down the causes of some of these little noises.

Often a loose part can be located by rapping with your knuckle on the instrument in various places. If you knock on the body and the noise appears to come from the neck, for example, then there's probably something loose on the neck or peghead. If the noise occurs only when you rap on the back, then there's probably a brace loose inside there.

THE TUNERS

When you're trying to locate a rattle, the headstock is an obvious place to start because things are screwed onto it. Almost every part of the tuner has the potential to come loose and start rattling. The nuts that screw down from the top have thin washers under them to protect the face of the headstock. They are screwed tight when the guitar is first assembled but may become loose because the wood compresses a bit. After the guitar is a few months old, it's a good idea to tighten these nuts a bit. Rattling washers are among the most common loose items on a guitar headstock.

Tuner buttons become loose for a variety of reasons. Sometimes the little retaining screws just back themselves out a little, and the button starts to rattle sympathetically at certain frequencies. Simply tightening the screw will fix this one nicely. Sometimes I need to drop a tiny bit of very thin acrylic glue onto the button shaft of the tuner to secure the little decorative collar. Even if it is almost imperceptibly loose, it can make a nasty noise when the instrument is played.

THE TRUSS ROD

Another less common place to check for rattles is the truss rod cover. Underneath the cover, the truss rod nut may also be loose, and it or the washer under it can make a lot of noise. Even if the angle of your neck is just right, it's generally a good idea to tighten the truss rod nut just enough to keep it from coming unscrewed and allowing the washer to become loose.

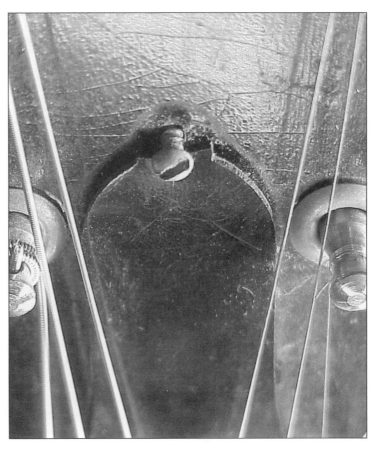

A loose truss rod cover can make noise.

The truss rod itself can graze the inside wall of its slot inside the neck and sing out loudly when you play just the right note. If you change the adjustment of the rod just a hair, you might keep it from rattling. The conventional repair for a rattling truss rod is to inject a bit of glue through a tiny hole drilled through the fingerboard down into the cavity that houses the truss rod. In skilled hands, this is a very safe procedure.

STRINGS AND TUNING POSTS

There is a special kind of buzz that is created if a string passes too close to a tuning post. You can avoid this problem by noticing how close each string comes to its neighboring post when you restring the guitar. If the design of the peghead won't allow enough clearance, then make sure the string rubs tightly against the post by winding it around a few extra times. Conversely, if the string just barely touches the neighboring post and is wound numerous times, you might be able to fix the problem by winding the string fewer times. The string should either miss the post altogether or be held against the post tightly enough so that it doesn't rattle.

A clumped-up mass of extra string at the peghead may have a casual or folksy look, but it can be a source of nasty noises. Cut the free end of the string short so it doesn't dangle and rattle or buzz. The strings themselves can have loose windings, particularly when they get old and worn. Loose windings make just about the worst buzzing noise you can get from an acoustic guitar!

NECK BOLTS

These days, lots of guitars feature bolted-on necks. On rare occasions, these bolts may be a bit loose, allowing the washers under them to make quite a lot of noise when the guitar is played. Simply tightening the bolts will make the problem go away.

THE TOP

By far the most active part of the guitar is its top. One of the more subtle top buzzes comes when a string is not properly seated and the windings snag between the bridge pin and the side of the hole, allowing the string to hang down inside the guitar. If the string ball is even just a little loose, it can rattle and buzz on every note. Some guitar

The problem might be as simple as dangling string ends at the peghead.

bridges have lots of screws and adjustable parts. Any of these parts can become loose and will rattle like crazy under the right circumstances.

Cracks, loose braces, and other structural damage is frequently the cause of buzzing or rattling. A brace doesn't have to be extremely loose to make nasty sympathetic noises. In fact, in most noisy braces, the looseness is almost imperceptible. It can take a trained luthier quite a while to locate some of these little fellows. Clearly, loose braces and cracks should be repaired whether they buzz or not, but often it's the buzzing that alerts us to the presence of such damage.

ELECTRONICS

On-board electronics are increasingly common in acoustic guitars. Adding a pickup means adding parts that can vibrate and make noise, especially if they become loose with time. Considering how the wires hang around inside an acoustic guitar, it's amazing that they don't rattle and buzz more often. If wires do rattle, keeping them quiet is a simple matter of adding little stick-on retainers to hold them in different positions. Electronic modules and controls, especially those with heavy batteries attached, are prone to rattling. Often, these rattles can be stopped with little pieces of tape or strategically placed bits of plastic foam.

Loose parts are not the only causes of rattles and buzzes. Low action, uneven frets, trouble at the nut or saddle, improper truss rod adjustment, and lots of other factors can also cause buzzing. Noises caused by loose parts are more likely to buzz all the time or only when you play certain notes. If you're having trouble locating the problem yourself, a good luthier should be able to take your guitar through a series of diagnostic techniques to help you locate the tiniest loose part.

RESONATOR RATTLES

Q *My resonator guitar has a strange rattle in it. Could my strings be too light, or could this be caused by the cone not being flat?*

A An improperly seated resonator would be a good guess. "Strange rattles" on resophonic guitars can also originate from the tailpiece, the machines, the nut or saddle slots, or the desiccated bodies of small invertebrates who got lost in there and starved or died of shock. The spider resonators found in most Dobros have a screw in the bridge saddle that can be tightened a little to snug the fit between the feet of the bridge and the resonator. On single- and triple-cone National guitars, the resonator cone(s) should be firmly seated against the well in which they are mounted. I once stopped a resonator buzz in my old National Triolian by pressing gently against the bridge saddle with the eraser end of a lead pencil! The use of glue or gaskets to improve the seating of the resonator is not recommended.

—Steve James

When Guitars Crack

Frank Ford

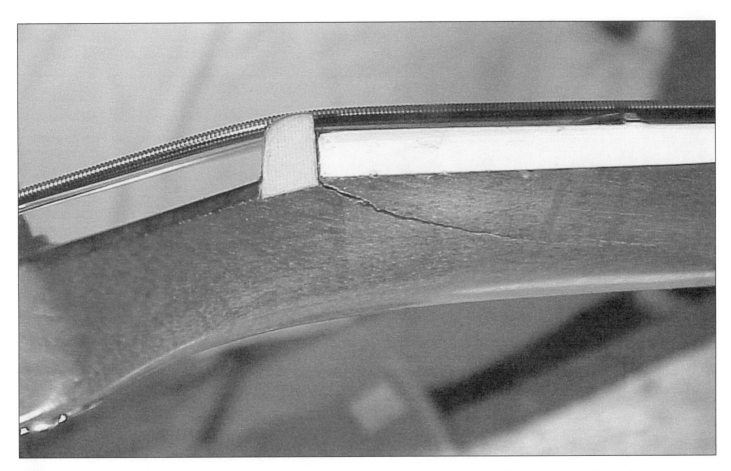

The classic neck crack.

got up from playing some tunes and made it about ten feet across the lawn at San Jose State before my guitar case flopped open and my D-28 bounced out on the ground. The grass was kind to me that day, and my guitar received nary a scratch. Since then, I've had 30 years of experience talking to guitar players about their accidents, and I've had a few more close calls of my own. Most of us are bound to make a slip now and again, and our instruments are likely to show the scars.

Flattop guitars are made with some of the widest and thinnest pieces of wood found in any stringed instruments, so they are particularly susceptible to cracking when they get bumped or leaned on. On top of that, guitars are likely to crack as their parts shrink when they dry out too much in high heat and/or low humidity.

Some cracks are benign and need no attention, while others are structurally significant and must be repaired immediately to avoid further damage. Strange as it may seem, cracks usually have little influence on the tone of a guitar.

Guitar bodies made of laminated woods may not sound as good as those made of solid materials, but they hardly ever crack. That's because there are three layers of wood veneer glued together with the grain running in different directions, like plywood. This discussion of cracks concerns solid-wood instruments only.

Your local luthier is the one to see when you notice a crack anywhere on your guitar. An experienced guitar mechanic will give you specific advice about possible repairs. But it pays to be well informed, so let's discuss some of the common types of cracks, their causes and significance, and how to avoid them.

This guitar top has split wide open because of shrinkage.

SHRINKAGE

When wood loses moisture, it shrinks in width and thickness, but not in length. If a guitar is moved to a much drier climate than that in which it was built, the wooden parts will shrink slowly, and tension will develop across the grain, often resulting in cracks. This shrinkage is just about the only cause of cracks in fingerboards. Fingerboard cracks are hardly ever structurally serious and need to be glued or filled only for cosmetic reasons.

Guitar sides don't often develop serious cracks from dryness. On most guitars, the sides are not braced across their width, so if they shrink with dryness, the guitar simply becomes imperceptibly thinner.

Tops and backs are vulnerable to shrinkage cracks because they are wide, thin, braced across their width, and supported rigidly all around their edges. Shrinkage cracks in tops or backs seldom threaten the longevity of a guitar, but gluing and reinforcing them with little patches inside the guitar is good protection against further damage. You can't tell by looking whether a top or back crack will cause buzzes, rattles, or other undesirable noises. Some really big cracks make no noise, and some really tiny ones vibrate like crazy! Noisy cracks obviously must be repaired, but quiet ones may often be left alone.

There's nothing like a hot parked car to generate heat, which will drive the moisture out of wood in a hurry. The kind of shrinkage that takes months to damage a guitar can happen in just a few hours at temperatures over 150 degrees Fahrenheit in a hot car. Plastic parts such as binding and pickguards shrink with heat and age and can also cause cracks in guitars as they shrink. In order to relieve the tension of a shrinking pickguard, the luthier must remove and reglue it.

Age, humidity, temperature, and accident can also cause cracks in the cosmetic elements of a guitar. Veneers, binding, purfling, inlay, and finish may crack, and these cracks have no significance to the life of the guitar. They may look pretty bad, but they don't cause structural or tonal problems.

BUMPS AND FALLS

Another common way that guitars get cracked is by being dropped. Some cracks follow the grain, while others cross the grain. Most cross-grain cracks are serious and should be reinforced inside to prevent further structural damage. If they are small and far away from the bridge or neck block, cross-grain cracks will not grow on their own, unless they are bumped again. But reinforcement is good insurance.

Some drops result in pieces of the wood actually breaking off. If the missing pieces can be found, the best repair job is usually to rebuild the area and reinforce the inside. A large wood inlay job is structurally sound but almost always unsightly. If the damage is severe enough, replacement of the entire side (or top or back) may be the only logical way to save an instrument.

SIDE CRACKS

Guitar sides are easily cracked by bumping into doorways or coffee tables, but the cracks usually have no effect on tone or longevity. But left unrepaired, side cracks usually spread and become longer. In the normal course of playing, a guitarist often leans on the guitar and may cause this kind of crack to spread. In fact, one of the most common causes of cracked guitar sides is normal playing. If you have a bunch of keys in your pocket and you lean on the instrument when you play, the bulge is likely to press the guitar side inward far enough to cause a crack.

Dreadnought guitar sides have a broad unsupported area that is most vulnerable to this kind of crack, and mahogany cracks the most easily. Side cracks should be glued together and reinforced inside with long vertical wood strips to keep the side from bending inward when pressed from the outside.

STRUCTURAL CRACKS

Inside the guitar, braces can crack, but only as a result of mechanical damage. Lean on the top or back too hard, or drop the guitar, and you might crack a brace. Cracked braces should always be glued back together to avoid progressive damage.

Neck cracks are almost always a result of an impact. Cracks at the heel and/or peghead are the most common sort of damage that occurs when a guitar is dropped in its case. (Airline baggage handlers have quite a reputation in this regard.) Neck cracks should be repaired as soon as possible. Release the string tension immediately to keep things from getting worse. It's always wise to pad the peghead of your guitar when you travel with it or ship it in its case. The peghead will be much less likely to crack if the case is bumped or even dropped.

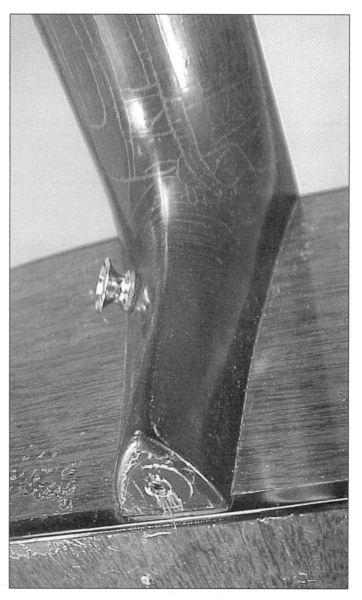

Cosmetic cracks cause no structural or tonal problems.

Bridges crack, too. A crack between the bridge pin holes is often a sign of weakness in the reinforcing bridge plate under the top of the guitar. A crack at the saddle is another sign that the bridge should be replaced. Most of the time the best bridge crack repair is actually bridge replacement. Bridges are under so much direct tension from the strings that any weakness is likely to cause failure.

REPAIR AND TOUCHUP

Crack repair usually means realigning the parts and clamping and gluing them back together. This may be particularly difficult in certain areas of the body, depending on access through the soundhole. Reinforcement of the repaired crack is a good idea when the stress that caused the crack is still present, as in top or back shrinkage. It's also wise to reinforce cracked areas where the impact or pressure is likely to happen again, as in the bunch-of-keys side crack.

Once the crack is repaired structurally, it's often desirable to retouch the finish in the affected area to make the crack less unsightly. Most of the time, the actual crack repair is less expensive and time consuming than the finish touchup.

It's a tough world out there, and cracks happen. If your guitar develops a crack, don't worry too much, but get some advice from a guitar repair specialist.

Bridge Repairs

Rick Turner

Willie Nelson's famous Martin N-20, before getting a new bridge.

The bridge on your acoustic guitar is one of the hardest working objects in show business. Not only does it have to transmit the vibrations of the strings to the sound-board, but it also has to withstand a constant pull of 140–180 pounds. Try walking around with a 150-pound briefcase for a while! It is no wonder that regluing bridges and working on the bridge area inside the guitar are very common procedures in repair shops.

Generally, luthiers glue bridges on with either hot hide glue (yes, the stuff made from animal hides and hooves) or with aliphatic resin glue sold commonly as yellow cabinetmakers' glue. While hide glue is the traditionalist's choice, most makers have switched over to the aliphatic type, which adheres well, is easy to work with, and has acoustic properties equivalent to hide glue. A properly glued line using fresh glue of either kind is stronger than the wood on either side of the joint. Either type of glue joint can be taken apart with judicious use of heat.

Heat is also the biggest enemy of guitar glue joints, particularly at the bridge. I learned this the hard way years ago when I was play-ing guitar with Canadian folksingers Ian and Sylvia. We were playing the Cellar Door in Washington, D.C., and we had a rent-a-car with a huge glass window instead of a trunk lid. My D-28 was on top of the luggage in the back and got the full brunt of the July sun. We got to the club for a sound check, and when I opened my guitar case the bridge was completely off. The temperature had probably reached 140 degrees inside the case, and the bridge glue joint was history. I borrowed another guitar while late mandolinist/singer John Duffy reglued the bridge for me, and all was well in a couple of days. Since then I myself have reglued bridges on several hundred guitars, and I'd say that overheating was the culprit at least 50 percent of the time. It can happen in attics, regular metal-lidded car trunks, and even to guitars left on stage in midsummer if it is hot enough. Bridge reglues due to heat stress are not consid-ered warranty work by manufacturers, so it is up to you to keep your guitar safe. I highly recommend using the ClimateCase cover over your hard-shell case if you will be spending much time at hot summer festivals.

Sometimes the bridge glue joint fails without any evidence of heat stress. This is harder to diagnose but can result from bad glue, improperly prepared glue surfaces, or even from too much clamp pressure forcing the glue out of the joint, a condition known in the wood industry as a starved glue joint. A good glue joint depends on both surfaces mating well without glue; only glues that have been formulated to be "gap filling" work well with ill-fitting parts, and such glues are not generally considered appropriate for glu-ing bridges on acoustic guitars.

So much for Diagnosis and Theory 101. Now, how do we deal with the problem? Unless a bridge has just a very slight lift where you can force in a bit of glue and reclamp, it is best to completely remove the bridge from the guitar before regluing it. This is not a job for amateurs. The bridge area is one of the first places a sophisticated potential buyer checks on a used/vintage guitar to see evidence of poor repair work, and it is very hard to camouflage shoddy work in this area.

I was once sent a beautiful 1917 Martin 0-18 with a rosewood pyramid-style bridge. The bridge had pulled up sometime in the past 20 years, and some total hack tried to force white silicone rubber tub sealant under the lifted back of the bridge while securing the bridge to the face with two wood screws—one a flathead and one a roundhead! Must have been some obscure bass-treble thing. I hate to say it, but this guitar is not the worst I've seen. Please, if your bridge is lifting, take it to a pro.

The first step in the process is to remove the bridge without losing any more wood than is absolutely necessary. I shine a heat lamp on the bridge to get heat through to the glue line. I first mask off the vulnerable top around the bridge with layers of aluminum foil and cardboard so as not to scorch it, and I brush a bit of lemon oil on the bridge to keep it from drying out too much. The oil also seems to carry the heat into the wood a bit faster. The trick here is not to slop on so much oil that it gets under the top finish or soaks the glue joint side of the bridge. When the bridge has heated up (the amount of time it takes differs with each instrument), I start probing around the perimeter of the bridge with a waxed blade made from a modified, very thin putty knife. I've rounded the two-inch–wide blade and sharpened it all around so I can rock it into the joint and pry very gently as I go. Certain places will let go easily, while other spots resist and need more heat. This is the most dangerous part of the bridge job for both the guitar and my hands; one of the worst cuts I've gotten in a guitar shop is from the edge of a bridge removal knife.

GRAIN RUN-OUT

One of the biggest problems at this stage of the job can be grain run-out guiding the bridge knife on a path right through the top. To understand this factor, you need to see the grain of the guitar top as having two planes. The obvious plane is evident by the vertical grain lines you see in the top. These are the tree's growth rings, which show alternating summer and winter growth patterns in wood that has been quartersawn. While straight grain in this pattern is a good sign in a guitar top, there is another plane—the plane of the guitar top itself—in which straight grain is extremely important to the strength of the wood. On a top with a lot of run-out, there will be a noticeable flash of color difference between the bass and treble sides as you change the angle of the top in a strong light. A top with little run-out will have much less flash. The flash is due to the differences in the refractive and reflective qualities of the two sides of the top due to the grain tilting one way on one side and the other way on the other side (see illustration, page 84). As you look straight at a top with run-out, the grain will point up and out on one side and down and out on the other.

Willie Nelson's famous Martin N-20, after getting a new bridge.

There are two problems with grain run-out in guitar tops. First, the wood is not as strong as when the wood fibers run perfectly parallel to the surfaces; but more to the point here, run-out can guide the bridge-parting knife right through the top itself, particularly if there is some really sticky glue at a critical point. This is one of the reasons for gently probing around the full perimeter of the bridge with the knife. By working with the grain from one side of the bridge on the treble side of the top and from the other side of the bridge on the bass side, it is possible to get the bridge off with minimal loss of wood.

An interesting side note: top grain run-out is more of a problem with vintage guitars than with more modern instruments because top wood split from the tree is easier to get these days than in years past when more wood was simply sawn. The splitting follows the grain nearly perfectly, minimizing run-out.

PREPPING THE BRIDGE AND TOP

Once the bridge is off, I let it and the guitar top cool off before continuing the work. If the bridge has warped in the process, I'll clamp it to a piece of aluminum to help it reform to its proper shape as it cools. But it does get tricky here: the bridge and top on older guitars will have slowly deformed together due to the pull of the strings, and the question is whether to try to flatten the top somewhat at this time or to preserve the now exaggerated curved line of the bridge-to-top joint. If the deformation of the top is excessive, it might be necessary to replace or reinforce the bridge plate, a usually trapezoidal reinforcing plate glued to the underside of the top in the bridge area. This is a tricky job made easier these days by miniature electric heating blankets made just for this job to help soften the glue. This kind of work is much like building a ship in a bottle since all the work has to be done through the soundhole. Some repairers, including Frank Ford of Gryphon Stringed Instruments, are using fiber optics, miniature lights, and video cameras to see what they are doing inside the guitar! It's a little like laparoscopic surgery.

When I'm satisfied with the shape of the top, it's time to prep the glue joint area. Any splinters or chunks of top wood should be replaced or spliced in so the top is as structurally sound as possible. This can get tricky, especially on guitars needing a second or third bridge reglue, which may have lost significant original wood. Even worse are plywood-topped guitars where the layers of wood are delaminating under the bridge. I worked on a black Yamaha APX 12-string for Carl Wilson of the Beach Boys. The guitar

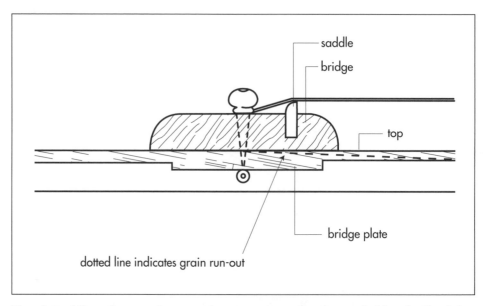

dotted line indicates grain run-out

The dotted line shows where grain run-out can lead your bridge knife right through the guitar's top.

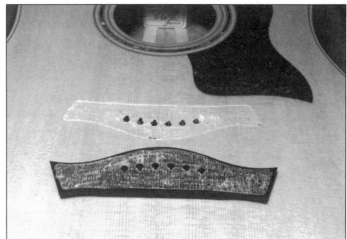

If you can slide a piece of paper under the bridge, it will need to be removed and reglued.

had baked on stage at a very hot gig. Not only was the bridge lifting off, but the plies of the top were delaminating. As an emergency repair, I flooded the voids with superglue and did as even a clamp job on the top as possible. It held for at least one more season!

This is also the time to look closely for any spots where the top may be pulling away from the braces. With X-braced guitars (most steel-strings), it's not uncommon to find an area or two at the ends of the bridge where the X passes under where the pull on the bridge has lifted the top from the braces. You can see this telegraphed through the top as a little bubblelike spot where the generally smooth and gentle curvature of the top is somewhat rippled. By forcing either hot hide glue or aliphatic resin glue into the gaps between the top and the brace and clamping overnight, the braces can be reglued.

REGLUING

Now comes the easy part. I spread a thin layer of aliphatic resin glue on both the bridge bottom and the area of the top where the bridge goes, and I align the bridge using a couple of plastic bridge pins. On classicals, I'll drill a couple of 16th-inch holes through the bridge under the saddle slot and into the top and then use toothpicks for alignment. I use a block of wood (a caul) to spread out clamp pressure on the underside of the top; it is shaped approximately like the bridge plate area and notched to fit over the braces. Five or six deep-throated clamps provide the pressure needed to evenly clamp the bridge to the top, and the bridge is protected from denting by leather-tipped mini-cauls. Since I've made sure that the fit is good, clamp pressure need not be excessive, assuring a good, even glue line.

After cleaning up any glue squeeze-out, I set the guitar aside, leaving it in clamps for 24 hours (I know they say three or four hours, but I prefer 24). I prefer not to string up the guitar for 48 hours, though in cases like making a new bridge and gluing it on to Willie Nelson's guitar, I had less than 24 hours to do the whole job. On that one, I strung it up one string at a time to check the action, and then it was out the door. It didn't come back, so I guess it's fine!

The final step is checking and adjusting action if necessary, refitting the pickup if there was one, and doing any final cleanup. Then the guitar is ready for its next (hopefully) 100 years.

Neck Resets

Rick Turner

There comes a time in the life of a steel-string guitar when the years of string tension have finally distorted the geometry of the instrument beyond what a simple adjustment of the action can fix. (You'd get bent, too, if you had to carry 150 to 180 pounds of tension around for 30 or more years!) As the various pieces of wood that make up the top, sides, and back of the guitar slowly deform, the string action rises ever higher, until the guitar gets to the point where reducing the height of the bridge and/or saddle is no longer a reasonable way to regain playability. That's when it's time to get a neck reset.

Many acoustic guitars are built with a bit of "extra" bridge and saddle height so a luthier can compensate for the distortion by lowering the saddle and/or shaving down the top of the bridge. Most steel-string acoustic bridges are about $^1/_4$ to $^5/_{16}$ of an inch high, with the saddle protruding about an eighth of an inch. If the action can be made right without deviating too far from these measurements, then you might be able to avoid a neck reset without compromising tone.

The string tension generally results in at least two visible effects: the guitar's top bellies up around the bridge, and the neck-to-body angle changes. In extreme cases, the top's upper bout can also start to cave in. A certain degree of top belly is considered normal for older steel-strings. Many of the best prewar Martins, for example, look a bit pregnant. I've heard it said at bluegrass festivals that older instruments that don't have a bit of

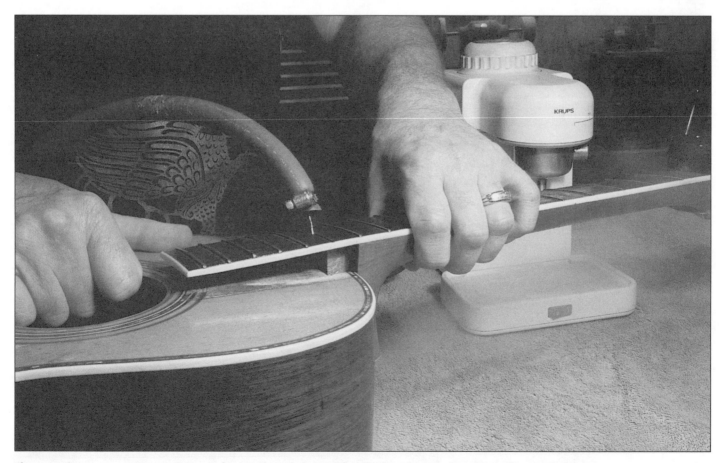

The repairer pumps steam into a dovetail neck joint to melt the glue and remove the neck intact.

bulge just don't have the tone either. There may be some truth to this statement, since a guitar that doesn't distort over time is probably overbuilt. But what we're really concerned with here is neck angle, and that is where we have the opportunity to make corrections, including compensation for top belly.

TO RESET OR NOT TO RESET

How do you know if a neck reset is indicated? I've seen a lot of guitars get diagnosed for resets that, in my opinion, weren't necessary. I tend to work on the conservative side of things: if the action can be made decent without shaving the bridge too low, I try to avoid the reset. It's kind of like making a call for angioplasty versus a heart bypass operation—either way it's a big deal, but one method is a bit less invasive.

If your guitar does need a neck reset, this repair is definitely in the "don't try this at home" category. Neck resets are standard procedure for the truly qualified luthier, but you don't want someone doing his first reset on your vintage dreadnought!

Although 95 percent or more of neck resets are executed to correct for bellying and forward neck shift, the occasional reset is used to correct the opposite condition, where the action is too low even with a very high bridge. This sometimes happens when an old guitar made for Hawaiian lap-style playing, like a Roy Smeck or a Martin Hawaiian, is converted to Spanish style. But let's assume for now that the neck resets are to solve the problem of an action that's too high on an instrument whose bridge is too low.

Done right, a neck reset will not only dramatically improve the playability of your precious instrument, but can also bring out the tone of the guitar. This is because as the guitar ages, the tonal properties of the wood get better while the neck-angle-to-body geometry gets worse. When you reset the neck, you can have the best of both worlds—great aged wood and proper geometry.

How does a reset affect value on a vintage instrument? First, a good neck reset done by an experienced luthier can be virtually undetectable on guitars whose necks and bodies were lacquered before final assembly. Second, a reset can make the difference between a great playing instrument and a wall hanger. As far as "vintage value" goes, I would much rather have a 1938 Martin herringbone D-28 with a good reset than the same guitar with a shaved bridge and bad action. I think that most vintage guitar dealers would agree with me on this. Steel-string guitars, as we know them, have barely been around for 100 years, so we are just now seeing the effects of age and use on them. Violinists are used to the idea that their instruments need rebuilding every now and then, and guitarists finally seem to be coming around to that attitude.

To determine whether or not a guitar needs a reset, I put a straightedge on the top of the frets and slide it down to the bridge. If there is no drastic rise in the fingerboard between the 12th and 16th frets, the straightedge should just about graze the top of the bridge ahead of the saddle or hit it no more than about .015 inches below its top. (This applies only to unmodified bridges and assumes that the bridge height was correct for the type of guitar in question.) If the straightedge meets the bridge any lower than this, the instrument probably needs a reset.

If you sight the tops of frets 1–14 and see that an imaginary line following that sight line will land in the body of the bridge, then yes, you need a neck reset. Some repair techs will pull frets, plane the fingerboard, and refret to try to take care of fingerboard rise, but this is only effective in mild cases and does not affect neck-to-body angle, which may also be incorrect.

Neck reset techniques have come a long way in the past 25 years, and luthiers share techniques freely. Gone are the days of guitar-making secrets passed down to the few and withheld from the many. If you bring your guitar in for a reset, here's what will probably happen to it.

DOVETAILED NECK

On guitars with dovetail neck joints, I take out the 15th fret or whichever fret is right over the dovetail joint. The fret should be heated to make removal easy and to avoid fingerboard chip-outs.

RESHAPING THE NECK

Q *The neck on my guitar is too fat for my tastes. Would it be possible to shave it down a bit without affecting the action?*

A There are several reasons for not reshaping the neck on your guitar. The first, of course, is that the neck may bow forward with medium strings, although it is sometimes possible to stiffen the neck by refretting with tighter frets. If the tang of the new frets (the part that goes into the fingerboard) is wider, the new frets will act as wedges, putting a reverse curve on the neck to counteract string tension.

Another reason not to modify your guitar is that unless the job is done carefully and the new finish perfectly matched to the original color, your instrument may be worth less than when you started. And if there is a warranty to the original owner, it would be voided by the modification. Your best bet is to buy or trade to get a guitar with an adjustable truss rod and low-profile neck.

—Richard Johnston

If the neck was joined to the body before finishing (which is common with Gibsons, Guilds, and Gibson-made Epiphones, for instance), the finish needs to be carefully cut at the sides of the heel in order to allow the neck to slide free. This is a tricky procedure that makes it much harder to do inconspicuous resets on guitars made this way. Martin, Santa Cruz, and Larrivée guitars, among many others, have their necks glued on after finish, making resets much easier to hide.

The next step is gently heating the part of the fingerboard that's over the body to soften the glue joint with the top. Applying lemon oil to the fingerboard will help transfer the heat through the board and prevent excessive drying and cracks. The idea here is to preserve the structural integrity of the fingerboard by not having to cut through a fret slot. I then loosen the fingerboard over the body by carefully slipping in a sharpened blade that looks much like a very thin, wide oyster knife. A bit of spray-on dry lubricant makes this step go easier.

Next, two holes are drilled through the fret slot down into the dovetail area. A basketball pump needle attached to a tube and steam source (I use a cappuccino steamer) introduces steam into the dovetail joint. The steam heat softens the glue in the dovetail, allowing the neck to be removed from the guitar's body.

There are a number of ways to actually remove the neck. I use a specially made jig that clamps to the guitar's body and has a screw that bears against the heel cap. After an average of two to five minutes of steam, the neck is ready to slide off, usually clean as can be. If there is any chipping of wood in the dovetail, I glue the pieces back immediately with aliphatic resin glue. Then I clean out any old glue, because new glue wants to stick to wood, not old glue.

I then carefully recut the surface of the neck heel that contacts the sides of the body on a taper from just under the fingerboard (where nothing is generally taken away) to the heel cap, establishing a new angle for the neck to be set to. This is usually done by hand, though luthier Steve Crisp has designed a clever jig into which the neck can be clamped with a tilting table to guide an offset router, which perfectly recuts the surface of the heel. Either way, the new angle is cut and then the dovetail is shimmed with veneers and refit to match the dovetail in the body.

BOLT-ON NECK

Many modern builders, Bill Collings, Dana Bourgeois, and Bob Taylor included, have chosen to bolt on the necks of their guitars, both as a manufacturing convenience and a way to make future neck resets much easier on the guitar and the luthier. As Taylor has pointed out, with a traditional dovetail joint, eight surfaces have to match up perfectly;

while with a bolt-on, the number is four, and only two of these have to be shaved to change the neck angle.

To reset a bolt-on neck, you only have to free the fingerboard and then release two bolts, which are usually hidden under a label on the neck block. Then it's just a matter of shaving the heel surface to get the new correct neck pitch and rebolting the neck while regluing the fingerboard to the top. Here too, the Crisp jig makes short work of cutting a new surface.

Whether your guitar has a dovetailed or bolted-on neck, a reset will generally change the plane of the fingerboard where it makes the transition from neck to top. If the fingerboard drops off drastically at the neck joint, it may be necessary to install a tapered shim to raise its end, and bound fingerboards complicate the procedure. If the fingerboard takes a rise over the body, the fingerboard will need to be planed level. Many repairers will not even do a reset without also doing a refret in order to correct the fingerboard surface, especially in the neck joint area. Sometimes we get lucky and no refret is needed, but don't be surprised if your luthier calls for the full job.

This area of the fingerboard over the guitar's top is problematic for many tradition-ally built acoustic guitars, and a number of modern instruments, such as the Martin D-1 and Steve Klein's guitars, attempt to beef up the support of the top under the fingerboard to alleviate these problems. Bob Taylor has written about how humidity changes can cause havoc in the neck-to-body fingerboard transition (see page 43); the top rises and falls as it expands and contracts in response to the rise and fall of ambient humidity. The fingerboard extension, being glued to the top, rises and falls too, and this can cause the action to go up and the strings to fret out at the same time. Try to keep your guitar safe from drastic humidity changes, and understand that if you have your action set up in either very high or very low humidity conditions, it will probably change drastically. Thus it is best to reset a neck under humidity conditions of around 43 to 48 percent.

After your guitar's neck has been reset and the instrument has been set up, you should experience the best of both worlds: the playability of a new neck angle and the sound of well-aged tonewood. Enjoy it.

Repairing and Restoring Vintage Instruments

Rick Turner

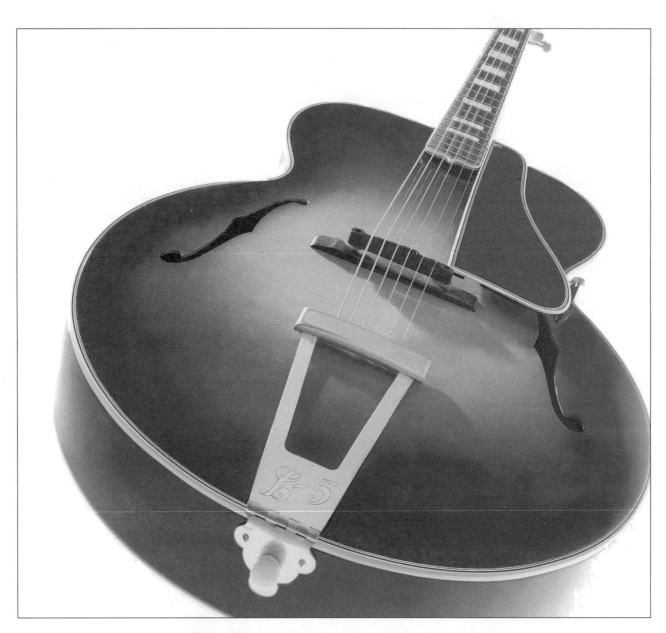

I n the world of vintage guitars, few subjects provoke more controversy than the repair and alteration of vintage instruments, which for the sake of this book I'll define as those that are more than 25 years old. In many fields of utilitarian collectible crafts, certain modifications are accepted and even encouraged, but guitar collectors seem to possess an almost maniacal attitude about instruments in original condition. Think *Spinal Tap,* folks. "Original tags! Don't even breathe on it!"

But in the real world, playing an instrument means inflicting wear on at least some of its parts. Play the strings and they will wear out. Each new set of strings will wear the frets, bridge saddle, nut, and tuner parts. So eventually the guitar will need a fret mill and setup. Then the nut will have to be recut because the first fret is lower, and the action is thus higher. After a few years of playing, the guitar will need a refret. Next, the guitar might need a new or shimmed nut, as the new frets require that the strings be raised back up closer to their original height. Now let's say you've got a Martin that is 35 or 40 years old. It's been refretted, maybe more than once, and it's getting that nice pregnant belly look they all get unless you're using very light strings. Also, the top, sides, and back have distorted after years of carrying a 150-pound load night and day, and the neck needs to be reset. Time to freak out? Not necessarily.

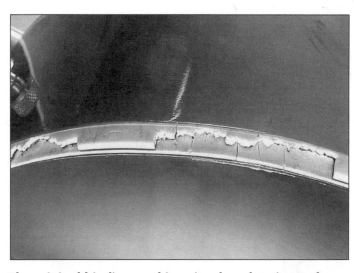

The original binding on this guitar has deteriorated.

Among some of the best vintage guitar dealers and restorers, including Dan Erlewine, Frank Ford, George Gruhn, and Hank Risan, there is a shared belief that eventually all high-performance acoustic steel-string guitars will need neck resets, not to mention refrets, new saddles, new nuts, tuner repairs, and perhaps much more work to keep them alive as musical instruments. The state of the art of fine guitar repair and restoration has reached an incredibly high level in the past 35 years, and good work should have no negative effect on the value of any guitars other than the very few truly mint instruments that have ceased to be usable and have achieved a kind of mythic icon status. In fact, many vintage instruments are now sold with the claim "Reset by T.J. Thompson" or some other well-respected luthier. Neck resets are part of the normal maintenance that keeps a fine guitar going decade after decade. You're still reaping the rewards of beautifully aged tonewood and you're adding to the package the proper body-to-neck geometry, allowing your guitar to benefit from the best of both worlds.

A questionable neck reset.

Many kinds of repair and restoration actually bring the guitar closer to the original intent of the designer. Even such iconic instruments as D'Angelico archtops can be improved upon in certain cases. D'Angelico himself was a master, but the supplier of his celluloid binding and pickguard material should have been jailed! There are fewer and fewer D'Angelicos with their original plastic parts; the celluloid was extremely unstable and basically self-destructed like a *Mission Impossible* audiocassette. A proper rebinding is practically a necessity with these instruments, and surely D'Angelico himself would not object if he were alive today.

ORIGINALITY

Another tricky issue to deal with when restoring vintage guitars is the use of original and vintage materials. Elephant ivory, tortoiseshell, whale baleen, and Brazilian rosewood are all politically incorrect materials nowadays, and aside from vintage pieces of raw or recycled material, their use is illegal as well. Antique stores abound in pieces made of these forbidden goods. Ivory sculptures, piano keys, and billiard balls, full tortoiseshells and carved objects, even old furniture is sometimes scavenged to provide pieces for restoration, but the penalties are high for illegal importation, trade, and use. Luckily, one usually needs only small pieces of these rare and sensitive materials, and there is a network of restorers and suppliers who deal in hard-to-find parts and supplies.

Sometimes you will find less than optimum original parts on an instrument. Many vintage collectible instruments were built in factories in the days when this meant a lot of hand work, but even a 100-year-old Martin is a factory-built guitar. This means that when necessary the wood used was the wood on hand, not always the very best available. After

Using hide glue to reglue a bridge.

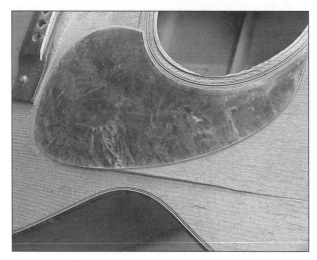

Tops are often cracked by shrinking pickguards.

all, they had payrolls to meet 100 years ago, too. Vintage dealer and restorer Hank Risan has no problem with the idea of selecting better than original wood for replacement parts, particularly for bridges. He goes through his vintage wood stash to select bridge blanks whose resonance matches his idea of what a particular guitar deserves. I have inlaid graphite bars in vintage instrument necks to keep them straight after a fingerboard replacement. On one Dyer harp guitar, I not only installed graphite but also replaced the original dyed pearwood fingerboard with ebony. The results were spectacular and totally in the spirit of the original builders, the Larson Brothers.

Original guitar finishes are one of the major hot spots in the discussion of vintage restoration. The ideal is a perfect untouched finish, but lacquer crazing (or cracking) is now considered acceptable even though it is due to a defect in the original material. If you look at late-19th-century guitars, particularly Martins, you will see finishes that are in a much better state of preservation than the finish on guitars of the 1930s, when sprayed lacquer became the standard. The older finishes were based on shellac, a hard natural excretion of the southeast Asian lac bug. Applied in hundreds of microthin coats in a technique known as French polishing, shellac is a miracle finish that ages remarkably well if it's not abused. Lacquer is much faster to apply, and it has supplanted French polish on all but handmade classical guitars. However, we now know that lacquer doesn't just dry to a cure and stop there; it continues over a long period of time to lose the plasticizers that make it flexible. The thin film shrinks, and as the lacquer gets more and more brittle it develops cracks like those in the muddy bottom of a dried-out lake. Is this a defect to be restored? For many years it was common to overspray old lacquer with fresh lacquer to try to hide the checking and perhaps refinish worn spots. Such overspray is almost always detectable and is now considered to be a bad idea. It is very hard to restore an oversprayed finish because the new lacquer partially melts the old while not blending completely because of finish formulation changes. Ironically, French polish makes an ideal lacquer finish restorative when used correctly, and the effects are reversible in the future should a more advanced concept of finish restoration be discovered. I recently restored the face finish on an early 1960s Guild Artist Award by treating the finish checks with a lacquer amalgamator that replasticized and melted the lacquer into the crackle zones, and then I went over the top with French polish, filling in the pick scratches. The end result was a restored finish that still looked very vintage, and it was done with materials that can be completely removed at any time in the future.

It is this concept of reversibility that has brought the best restorers in the business back to using materials common in the 18th and early 19th centuries. Log onto Frank Ford's incredible Web site at www.frets.com and read his treatises on both French polish and hide glue, the stuff that has held King Tut's furniture together all these 3,000 years.

Hide glue is a collagen protein gelatin derived from animal skin, bones, and hooves—sorry about that, but this isn't for vegetarians! Hide glue's biggest disadvantage is that you need to learn how to use it—the best stuff doesn't just squirt out of a bottle, it must be mixed fresh and used hot. The advantages are many and include strength, creep resistance, and the ease with which glue joints can later be disassembled with judicious use of heat, steam, and alcohol. Hide glue is the substance used to hold together virtually every stringed instrument classified as vintage, and it is the only glue that should be used to restore most older guitars. If you have a vintage piece you want restored, make sure your luthier understands how to use hot hide glue.

The simple act of stringing a vintage instrument also needs to be carefully addressed. Most parlor guitars, for instance, were originally strung with gut, and the Martin factory didn't make steel strings a factory option until the 1920s. Modern tastes have moved toward steel strings, and even extra-light strings can exert a greater load on delicate tops than the instruments were designed for. You might want to consider silk-and-steel, extra high–tension nylon, or some of the other specialty strings made to give a brighter sound to old guitars.

THE BOTTOM LINE

The cost of fine restoration has increased as skill levels have improved, so it is easy to spend as much as a guitar is worth just to make it playable. Where do you draw the line? When do you go with cheap and dirty repair work? Get an estimate on the work to be done and an idea of how your luthier plans to approach the job. There are always several ways of doing a particular procedure, and sometimes you just have to choose the easy way. Let's say the typical neck reset costs $350. Do you put that money into a 1959 Harmony Sovereign you bought for $300? If you just love the guitar, do it. What about that cool Silvertone with all the cracks in it? Go with a quick and dirty superglue and Titebond repair job and enjoy the guitar. What if you have a 1929 Martin 00-28, and you can't afford to spend the $600 needed for a reset, refret, crack repair, and finish touch-up? Don't go with a cheap job! Take the strings off the guitar and put it away until you can afford to get it done right, or else sell the guitar to someone who can afford to get it done right. Only you can say whether a particular repair job will be worth your money, but try to make informed choices. At least make sure that any quick and cheap jobs don't cause future restorers to curse the day you got the instrument. There are few things we repairers like less than coming across a butcher job on a great instrument.

Those guitars that are presently considered to be collectible or musically important as well as those that may be considered so in the future should be treated with respect. But do not hesitate to have necessary repair work done correctly for fear of hurting the "vintage value." Remember that in the world of vintage violins, 99 percent of the great instruments have been repeatedly repaired and restored in order to keep them in playing condition. That level of sophistication is coming into the world of fine guitars, and we now recognize that to play a musical instrument is to wear it out to some degree. The luthier's job is to build fine modern instruments and to keep the best of the vintage pieces healthy.

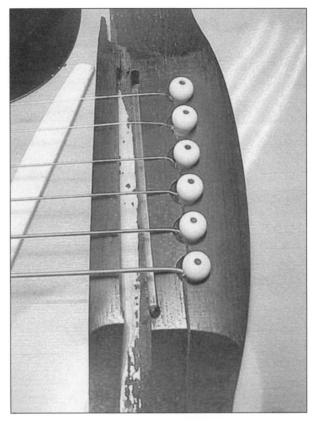

A cracked bridge.

Installing and Troubleshooting Pickups

Rick Turner

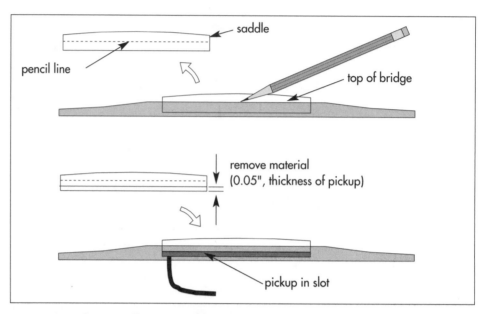

Instructions for installing an under-saddle pickup.

MOUNTING PICKUPS

Q *I'm concerned about drilling holes in my guitar for the sake of mounting a bridge pickup. What will installing one do to the tone, volume, and possible resale value of my instrument?*

A I generally tell my customers not to put pickups into their most precious acoustic guitars if they are at all concerned about changing the instruments. I also advise them to go ahead and do it if they really want to use the instruments on stage in situations where a mic just won't do. It is very reasonable to have two or more instruments. Use one for stage performance and preserve the best for purely acoustic playing. As for tone and volume, I've been involved in putting bridge pickups in hundreds of guitars and have heard only one complaint of tonal change. A well-installed pickup will not affect the structural integrity of the instrument.

—Rick Turner

One of the great paradoxes of the acoustic guitar is that for anything beyond the most basic back porch or living room use you need amplification. Acoustic guitars just aren't very loud. The hunt for solutions goes back to the early 1920s with Lloyd Loar's experiments in amplifying guitars and basses using electrostatic pickups. Ironically, Loar's fervent belief in the future of amplified musical instruments led to his departure from Gibson, whose controlling executives thought there was no future in electric guitars.

Today, aside from simply playing into a microphone, there are three basic technologies for amplifying guitars: under-saddle pickups (usually piezo-based), magnetic pickups, and surface vibration transducers. Each of them uses a device that transforms guitar string or top vibrations into electrical signals. Pickups are sometimes augmented with internally mounted microphones, which can be blended (either internally or externally) with the pickup signal to give a more natural and airy sound.

If you bought a guitar with a pickup already installed, you are mostly home free in terms of having to deal with tricky installation procedures. However, it might be worth knowing how pickups are installed in order to troubleshoot common problems. If you are adding a pickup to an existing guitar, there are a number of things you should know, and knowing them will probably send you to your nearest luthier for installation. I will not provide complete installation instructions here, but rather point out some highlights and some common problems to look out for.

MAGNETIC PICKUPS

Magnetic pickups depend on the ferrous part of a string interacting with a magnet and coil(s) in the pickup to generate a small electrical current that is an analogue of the string movement. Thus, magnetic pickups are not for the nylon-string player but only work on steel and steel-cored strings. Most aftermarket magnetic pickups mount to the edges of the soundhole of the guitar through some arrangement of clips or clamps and are very easy for a user to install—especially those pickups that have a dangling lead wire attached, such as Dean Markley pickups. Magnetic pickups can be extremely feedback resistant; the downside is that they can sound like electric guitar pickups, with the kind of midrange coloration more commonly associated with solid-body guitars. I have noticed that a lot of people who favor magnetic pickups on acoustic guitars play bottleneck slide; I suspect there is a kind of synergy between the magnetic pickup sound and the note range of most slide licks.

A more permanent installation requires reaming or drilling out the hole in the endblock of your guitar in order to install an endpin jack. This must be done very carefully or you'll split the endblock or sides of your guitar. I use a modified drill bit on which the rake angle of the tip has been reground to zero; an unmodified bit can grab the wood and tear the drill out of your hands with sometimes disastrous results.

The biggest problem with magnetic pickup installations is string balance. The magnetic load of strings made of plain steel is unequal to that of brass- or bronze-wound strings with steel cores. In the electric guitar world, musicians tend to use nickel or stainless steel wound strings, which have magnetic properties that balance out throughout the set. Acoustic strings are usually wound with either brass or bronze, which tends to dampen the magnetic response of the strings.

On most magnetic pickups, string balance is fixed and can only be changed with adjustments of pickup tilt, which affects the balance between the bass strings and the treble strings. Some pickups, including the Sunrise, have individual pole pieces, which can be used to tweak string-to-string levels. I find that most Sunrise users back the high B and E pole pieces way down into the pickup to prevent the plain steel strings from overpowering the bronze- or brass-wound strings.

Another caveat with installing magnetic pickups is possible damage to the rosette area of the guitar. Repeatedly installing and taking out a pickup may scratch the finish and even damage the soft top wood, and heavier pickups can really wreak havoc with delicate guitar tops if they are subjected to even normal on-the-road handling. The manual that comes with the Sunrise even suggests removing the pickup when transporting the guitar, and I've had to repair several guitars with rosettes badly damaged by the weight of the pickup stressing the soundhole area.

SOUNDBOARD TRANSDUCERS

Soundboard vibration transducers have a checkered past and uncertain future due to the difficulty of finding the sweetest of all spots—the microcosmic point on the guitar's top that represents the totality of guitar vibration. The problem is that different parts of the top move differently at different notes and harmonics, and very few places on the top represent a sum of the sound field, which really only comes together about five feet away from the guitar.

PLACING INTERNAL MICS

Q *I have an internal mic and a saddle pickup installed in my guitar. Where should I mount the mic?*

A Mic placement inside a guitar is weird science. There are no rules other than: "Try It. Like it? Do it!" I sometimes shock-mount mic capsules in a block of acoustically transparent foam rubber (open cell) and use double-stick foam tape to mount that to either the top or back of the guitar. This keeps weight to a minimum as well as reducing noise mechanically transmitted to the mic. Clamping any weight to a top brace will affect the sound of the guitar, but if it gives you the results you are looking for, who cares! As far as I'm concerned, anything goes with the guitar you are going to use for performance, especially if it isn't a precious collectible. Drill holes in it, put gaffers' tape over the soundhole, paint it silver, do whatever it takes to make it work for you.

—*Rick Turner*

ARCHTOP PICKUPS

Q *What kinds of pickups would work in my acoustic archtop?*

A There are fewer options available for amplifying acoustic archtops than there are for flattop guitars. The most important question to ask yourself is whether you're in search of a true acoustic sound or a more electric sound, which most people associate with archtop guitars in a jazz context. If it's the guitar's natural acoustic sound that you're after, be prepared for a bit of experimenting—unless you simply decide to use an external microphone. External mics work better with archtops than they do with flattops because archtops project more and have a less bass-heavy sound. Fishman Transducers and Shadow are the only companies I know of that make piezo pickups for archtops. These passive pickups are integrated in a replacement bridge, enabling installation without modifications to the instrument.

Many players successfully use miniature microphones (such as those made by Countryman and Crown) clamped into one of the f-holes. These can either be used exclusively or in conjunction with a pickup via a blending device.

If you're craving a more electric sound, you should probably look into a floating magnetic pickup, which mounts to the end of the fingerboard. Many people swear by vintage DeArmonds, which are increasingly difficult to find. Luckily, there are a few modern-day solutions available. Archtop builder Robert Benedetto markets his own design, and it has become a popular choice. Bartolini Pickups offers its 5-J, which features the same dimensions as the original Johnny Smith pickup. Shadow makes the Attila Zoller model, and EMG offers a pickup for those who prefer an active design.

—*Teja Gerken*

The best soundboard transducer I've heard is the old FRAP pickup and its more modern successor, the Trance Audio Acoustic Lens. Technically speaking, these are piezoelectric three-axis accelerometers, which react to all the subtle variations of vibration at the point where they are attached. The best-sounding installations are done with two pickups, both glued to the underside of the bridge patch directly under the saddle. There is considerable voodoo involved in the installation, and moving the transducer as little as a sixteenth of an inch can make a tremendous difference in the sound. To top it all off, the preferred glue takes 48 hours to cure, and the job must be done with absolutely no bubbles in the adhesive. So you don't know if the job is just right for two days, and if it isn't, you get to do it all over!

There are many other makes and styles of vibration transducers that can be readily affixed to the outside of a guitar top with results I can only describe as barely adequate. Tone tends to be very ragged, with massive peaks and valleys in the frequency response, and these pickups can be feedback monsters when attached to resonant tops. Though use of equalization can tame some of the problems, it introduces a whole new set of problems.

UNDER-SADDLE TRANSDUCERS

Under-saddle transducers are currently the most common type of pickup being used to amplify acoustic guitars. First popularized by Ovation, saddle pickups are now factory-installed on practically every guitar brand you can name. The aftermarket for this style of pickup has become huge, with Fishman, L.R. Baggs, Highlander, EMG, B-Band, and many others elbowing one another for space in guitar shop accessory counters.

The most common technology for under-saddle pickups is either piezo ceramic or one of the more flexible piezo plastic or rubber materials, which develop an electric charge when they are stressed. The B-Band pickup works on the electret principle but still senses vibration at the under-saddle position, a place in the guitar with its own particular sound. Virtually all under-saddle pickups must be used with an impedance-matching buffer preamp, often sold as an integral part of the pickup.

The advantages of under-saddle pickups are that they are relatively resistant to feedback, they are virtually invisible except for controls, and they can be installed and tweaked to get very credible sound. Electronics packaging has reached an incredible level of sophistication and miniaturization, and several companies now offer an integrated output jack/preamp chassis with their pickups.

While there are subtle differences among the various types of under-saddle pickups and differences among the preamps used with them, they're in the same position, and that position has a particular sound of its own. The pickup actually senses the string and saddle vibration before the top does, giving these transducers a very "in your face" kind of sound.

Under-saddle pickups are incredibly sensitive to the particular geometry of the individual guitar and the techniques used by the installer. The most common problem is string-to-string output balance. About 95 percent of the problems with these pickups can be traced back to either the original installation or to movement of the guitar top and bridge due to humidity changes. The latest generation of under-saddle pickups are sensitive along the entire saddle slot, and they are much better than the older six-spot types, but it is still best to have an experienced luthier with a whole bag of tricks do the installation.

The trick is to get absolutely even pressure along the length of the pickup, particularly directly under the strings. I visualize a kind of pyramid of pressure, with the top of the pyramid at the point where the string contacts the saddle. By ensuring that the pressure is evenly distributed from each string down to the pickup, you can get reasonable string-to-string volume. This isn't as easy as it seems; I find that minor variations of one or two thousandths of an inch in either the saddle slot or the bottom of the saddle can make much more of a difference to the amplified sound than to the acoustic sound of the guitar.

There are several voicing tricks used to equalize string response. Push back and down on the saddle to keep it from hanging up on the front wall of the saddle slot. It helps to have the saddle be a medium slip fit, even in humid weather. Cut the slots upward from the bottom of the saddle or use one of Fishman's Cleartone saddles, which are better able to flex along the contour of the saddle slot bottom. Add tiny bits of copper foil tape to the saddle bottom to increase the pressure under specific strings. Make slight cuts in the saddle bottom to tame a loud string.

The best installations I've done have been with a new saddle slot cut with the saddle tilting back toward the bridge pins at an angle of about eight to ten degrees. This modification allows the saddle to more nearly split the break angle of the string passing from the pin hole over the saddle, and it allows the pickup to download better.

Another trick is to determine if the guitar top bellies up significantly under string load. This can be measured with a special jig and a dial indicator. If the top does pull up, then the luthier can install a temporary internal jack under the bridge to artificially re-create the top distortion. With the top in the shape it takes under tension, the luthier can recut the saddle slot with the bottom as flat as it will be when the guitar is strung.

If you are going to install a pickup in your existing guitar, get as much information from the various manufacturers as you can. Listen to guitars that are similar to your own and are fitted with different kinds of pickups. Then get the advice of your local luthier, who deals with these devices on a daily basis. You may be better off going with your luthier's favorite pickup rather than the one with the biggest ads or wildest claims. A second-choice pickup installed correctly will outperform the latest, hottest, most acoustic pickup incorrectly installed every time.

AMPLIFYING A RESONATOR GUITAR

Q *Any words of advice about the best way to amplify a resonator guitar for live performance in clubs and coffeehouses?*

A In a live situation, a single directional microphone placed fairly close to the treble side of the cover plate should do the trick. The workingman's rig is a Shure SM-57. If you want to get fancy, try using something like an AKG 414 or a Neumann U 64. These are expensive and fragile, and I consider them more appropriate for a studio than a club date.

I've fitted a couple of my Nationals (a 1936 wood-body Trojan and my 1998 custom-style EN) with Highlander IP-1X pickups. I find that using the direct signal from the Highlander in combination with a microphone gives me a realistic resonator sound with plenty of volume and high end in situations like large rooms and festival stages where sound-check time is limited and feedback can be a problem. (I've gotten a lot of positive comments on the Highlander from audience members and sound techs alike.)

—Steve James

SIGNAL PROBLEMS WITH SADDLE PICKUPS

Q *The signal from my under-saddle pickup is uneven, with some strings sounding louder than others, and the shallower saddle that came with it is leaning over and causing intonation problems. What should I do?*

A It sounds like your pickup is the kind with six tiny piezo-electric crystals that sense string vibration. It is critical that these crystals line up directly under each of the strings. If your guitar has string spacing other than what is standard, you will need to purchase a custom pickup. I have found that a pickup misalignment as little as $3/32$ of an inch is noticeable. Also, it is essential to have equal down pressure on each of the six crystals from the strings down through the saddle in order to have equal output for each string.

Voicing problems with pickups that are sensitive along their full length, including Highlander, Fishman Matrix, EMG, Baggs Ribbon, and B-Band, tend to be with the high and low E strings. This is also because of uneven saddle pressure on the pickup and can be caused by improper installation or humidity changes.

Sometimes I split the saddle into two sections to better equalize the down pressure. Or you might consider the Fishman Cleartone saddle. As for your leaning saddle, this is not good for several reasons: Intonation suffers, string pressure on the pickup is likely to be uneven, acoustic and electric tone can be inhibited, and the saddle can hang up during a string change, resulting in total loss of contact with one or more crystals. The saddle slot should be grooved lower and a new saddle fitted so the action and intonation are correct. Saddle fit with pickups is a delicate art. Take your guitar to a competent repairer to get the job done right.

—Rick Turner

A Complete Glossary of Acoustic Guitar Lingo

Richard Johnston

0, 00, 000 Guitar body size designations derived from C.F. Martin. At first Martin's largest guitar was size 1, with numbers 2 through 5 denoting progressively smaller sizes. A larger body was introduced in the 1850s, called a size 0, later followed by the even larger 00 in the 1870s (the 00 is about the size of a typical classical guitar). The 000, considered small today, was the largest Martin until dreadnoughts (D size) were introduced. These shapes were changed in the early 1930s when Martin went to designs with 14 frets clear of the body.

12-FRET/14-FRET This describes the number of frets clear of the guitar's body, not the total number of frets on the fretboard. If the guitar has a cutaway, you count the frets clear of the noncutaway side.

12-STRING A double-strung guitar; an instrument with six pairs of strings. The treble pairs (high E and B) are usually tuned in unison, and the rest are tuned in octaves, although some players also tune the third pair of strings in unison.

ACOUSTIC-ELECTRIC An acoustic guitar with a pickup for playing through an amplifier.

ACTION The height of the strings above the fretboard. A guitar with high action is harder to play than a guitar with low action, but low action will produce more fret buzz if you strum hard.

ARCHTOP A guitar in which the soundboard is carved or pressed into an arched shape, higher in the center where the bridge is located. The design is derived from violin-family instruments, and today's archtop usually has two S-shaped soundholes, although round or oval soundholes were used on early versions.

BELLY BRIDGE A guitar bridge with a bump, or belly, behind the bridge pins, which allows more gluing surface to the top. C.F. Martin began using this design in 1930, a few years after the company switched from gut strings to steel strings on most models. Gibson adopted a similar design years later but reversed it so the belly was in front of the saddle.

BINDING Inlaid strips that protect and decorate the edges of the guitar's body and/or neck. Wood and plastic are most common today, though ivory and tortoiseshell were sometimes used on high-grade instruments in the past.

BISCUIT A small disc of wood mounted on top of the cone in a resonator guitar, such as a National. Because these instruments do not have a conventional guitar's bridge, the saddle is mounted in the biscuit.

BLOND Refers to a clear or natural finish on light-colored instrument woods, such as maple or spruce, as opposed to a stained surface or a shaded, sunburst effect that darkens the wood at the instrument's edges.

BOLT-ON NECK A guitar neck that is bolted to the body, as opposed to a neck fastened to the body with a glued dovetail joint.

BOOK-MATCH The right and left sides of most wooden instruments are made of matching pieces of wood. By using thin boards cut in succession from a thicker piece, the right half of a guitar's back or top can be a mirror image of the left half.

BOUT The portion of a guitar defined by the sides' convex curves. The upper bout is generally smaller than the lower bout, and between them is the more narrow portion, called the waist.

BRACING Thin strips of wooden reinforcement glued to the top and back of the guitar. A series of horizontal bars, such as on the back of a guitar, is called ladder bracing. Steel-string guitar tops usually have a pattern in which the two main braces intersect just below the soundhole, called X-bracing. Fan bracing is a series of braces spread out beneath the bridge, most often seen on classical guitars. Many guitars have top bracing that is a combination of two or more of these patterns.

BREAK ANGLE The angle a string makes when passing over the bridge saddle to the bridge pin hole, or over the nut to the tuning machine. A steep angle bends the string more sharply and may contribute to string breakage. Too shallow a break angle may hamper tone, allowing the string to vibrate across the saddle or nut like a sitar string. Break angle also affects output from an under-saddle pickup.

BRIDGE A wooden support for the saddle to which the strings are secured. When strings attach to a tailpiece fastened to the bottom of the guitar (as on archtops), the bridge is not glued and is little more than a floating support for the saddle. On most flattops, both steel- and nylon-string, the bridge is glued to the soundboard.

BRIDGE PINS Small, tapered pegs of plastic, wood, or metal that anchor the string balls at the bottom of the holes in the bridge.

BRIDGE PLATE A wide, flat brace under the bridge. If the guitar has a pin bridge, the bridge plate is usually made of hardwood to better withstand damage from the string balls. Archtops and other guitars with floating bridges usually do not have bridge plates, and classical guitars often don't.

BUZZ The noise created when a vibrating string is striking frets between the fretted note (or the nut) and the saddle.

CLASSICAL GUITAR A nylon-stringed guitar often used to play classical music, generally with a flat fingerboard about two inches wide at the nut and a pinless bridge to which the strings are tied.

CNC Computer numerical control. A sophisticated machine that is capable of many different operations and is controlled by a computer. Usually used for milling the guitar's many wooden parts, including necks and bridges.

COMPENSATED SADDLE A saddle shaped to move the contact point for each string slightly forward or back to allow better intonation.

COVER PLATE The round metal cover fastened to the face and covering the cone(s) of a resophonic guitar such as a National or a Dobro.

CUTAWAY Describes a guitar body from which a U-shaped portion of the upper bout has been removed to allow easier access to the frets that are over the body. A Florentine cutaway has a sharp point, while a Venetian cutaway is rounded.

DOBRO A type of resonator guitar, invented in the late 1920s, in which the saddle is mounted in a cast aluminum "spider" or grid, which spans an inverted cone of spun aluminum. The term was once used only to refer to instruments made by the Dobro Company, which held the trademark, but is now commonly used to describe any such resonator guitar. *See* National

DOT NECK Guitar fretboard with simple dots for position markers instead of larger, more elaborate inlays.

DOVETAIL Hindquarters of a peace activist, especially a folksinger. More often refers to a woodworking joint used to fasten the neck to the body of the guitar.

DREADNOUGHT A large, deep-bodied guitar with a wide waist. Martin took the name from a heavy British battleship, the HMS Dreadnought, when the first dreadnought was built in 1916.

ENDBLOCK The large block inside the body of a guitar where the sides come together in the center of the lower bout. On steel-string guitars there is generally a hole for mounting the endpin or strap button.

ENDPIN JACK A special quarter-inch phone jack, with an outer flange for mounting a strap, which replaces the endpin on acoustic-electric guitars.

ENDPIN A wooden or plastic pin to which a strap can be attached. It has a tapered shaft that fits into a hole in the bottom of the guitar. *See* endblock

FAN BRACING *See* bracing

F-HOLES The *S*-shaped soundholes on an archtop instrument, usually placed in the soundboard just below the waist, on either side of the bridge.

FINGER REST The elevated celluloid platforms supplied with early archtop instruments were described as finger rests because they compensated for the extreme distance between the soundboard and the strings. Today such elevated finger rests are usually called pickguards.

FINGERBOARD Also called a fretboard. A thin piece of hardwood, most often ebony or rosewood, glued to the upper surface of the neck and usually continuing over the soundboard to the soundhole. Frets are wedged or glued into slots in the fingerboard.

FINISH A thin protective coating. On musical instruments it is usually shellac, varnish, or lacquer. *Satin* refers to a finish with low gloss.

FLATTOP A guitar with a thin soundboard of even thickness, braced on the underside to withstand string tension. The bridge is glued to the soundboard, which usually has a round soundhole. The term typically refers to a steel-string guitar, even though classical guitars also have flat tops.

FLORENTINE CUTAWAY *See* cutaway

FRENCH POLISHING The ancient method of applying a highly polished shellac finish by rubbing it onto the surface with a wad of cloth, using a small amount of oil as a lubricant.

FRETBOARD *See* fingerboard

GOLPEADOR A tap plate or pickguard on a classical or flamenco guitar. (*Golpe* means *tap* in Spanish.)

GRAND CONCERT A better-than-average public performance. More often refers to a guitar about the size of a Martin 00 or a classical guitar.

GUIT-JO Contraction (vernacular only) of *guitar-banjo,* which is an instrument with a banjo body and a guitar neck.

GUT-STRING GUITAR A pre–World War II instrument built for strings made of sheep intestines. After the war, nylon strings became widely available.

HARDWARE The metal parts that are fastened to a guitar, as opposed to portions that are integral to the guitar itself. On an archtop, the hardware includes tuners, tailpiece, bridge, pickguard, and pickup(s).

HAWAIIAN GUITAR A guitar whose strings are high above the fretboard, which is played horizontally on the lap, using a steel bar in the left hand. Until recently *Spanish guitar* was used as *Hawaiian guitar*'s antonym, to refer to any guitar played in the conventional fashion. Today most people think of a classical instrument with nylon strings when they hear *Spanish guitar.*

HEADSTOCK The top of the guitar's neck, where the strings are fastened to the tuning machines or pegs. Also called the peghead.

HEEL The portion of the guitar's neck that fastens to the body.

HERRINGBONE A type of wood marquetry or purfling often used by C.F. Martin from the 1850s through 1946, and again from 1976 to the present. The design is formed of two rows of alternating dark and light chevrons that resemble a miniature strip of herringbone-patterned fabric. A key identifying feature of style 28 Martin guitars.

HIGH-STRUNG GUITAR Most often used for playing rhythm, a high-strung guitar has its top two strings tuned like a regular guitar, while the bottom four (E, A, D, and G) are tuned an octave above normal, as on a 12-string.

INLAY A decorative veneer of pearl, metal, or wood glued into a matching recess. On musical instruments such as guitars, inlays are usually found on the fretboard and peghead, and less commonly on the bridge and heel.

INTONATION A guitar's ability to yield notes of accurate pitch as you play up the neck. Poor intonation may be caused by inaccurate fret placement (which is rare in production guitars) but most often is the result of an improperly compensated saddle, which fails to correct the sharping effect created by pushing the strings down to the frets.

JUMBO Gibson once called all its large flattops "jumbos," but today the term usually describes a 17-inch wide guitar with a shape characterized by a round lower bout and a narrow waist.

LADDER BRACING *See* bracing

LAMINATED WOOD Wood whose thickness is made up of thin layers of veneer glued together, as in plywood. Solid wood is only one, thicker layer.

LAP STEEL Years ago both *lap steel* and *steel guitar* referred to a guitar with strings high off the neck, played horizontally on the lap using a steel bar to "fret" the strings. Today *lap steel* usually means a small, solid-body electric built for playing this style, while *steel guitar* refers to the next evolutionary step, the eight- or even ten-string electric table with detachable legs, which often has two or more necks in different tunings. Next came the *pedal steel,* with knee levers and foot pedals.

LUTHIER Someone who makes musical instruments.

MACHINE HEADS The right-angle geared tuners commonly found on guitars. Also called tuning machines.

NATIONAL A type of resonator guitar, invented in the late 1920s, where the saddle is mounted on top of one or more inverted cones of spun aluminum. Although the name refers to the original company that held the patents, the term is now commonly used to refer to any resonator guitar of this type, as opposed to the Dobro style. *See* Dobro

NECK ANGLE The angle at which the neck intersects the body of the guitar. On a flattop guitar, a low or shallow neck angle (with the fretboard roughly parallel to the soundboard) means that the guitar's bridge and saddle must be quite low for the strings to be close enough to the frets and that the strings will be close to the soundboard as well. A steep neck angle results in a tall bridge and/or saddle.

NECK RELIEF A slight forward curve in the neck. Many players prefer to play on a neck that is not perfectly straight, and a slight amount of neck relief often allows more aggressive playing in the lower positions without fret buzz.

NECK RESET Removing the neck from the body and altering the joint so that when the neck is reattached, string action is optimal with a bridge and saddle of normal height. *See* neck angle

NUT Term of endearment often directed at musicians. Also the upper string bearing at the top of the fingerboard, which is usually made of bone or hard plastic. Strings pass through the notches in the nut on their way to the tuning machines.

NYLON-STRING GUITAR A term that used to refer only to the classical guitar. Today, many acoustic-electric guitars have nylon strings, including some with solid bodies. *See* classical guitar

ORCHESTRA MODEL Today this phrase is generally used to describe a 000-size guitar with 14 frets clear of the body (Martin's first modern flattop, introduced in 1929). In the 1930s and '40s, Martin called all of its flattop guitars with 14-fret necks "orchestra models."

PARLOR GUITAR A small 12-fret guitar, especially one from the 19th or early 20th century, when gut strings—not steel—were standard.

PEGHEAD *See* headstock

PICKGUARD A thin piece of plastic or wood glued to the soundboard to protect it from scratches. The elevated version on archtops, once called a finger rest, is now called a pickguard as well.

PIN BRIDGE A bridge in which the strings are anchored in holes that go through the bridge and soundboard. The small ball at the end of each string is held in place just beneath the top of the guitar by small bridge pins.

PURFLING Usually refers to thin strips of wood or plastic used as decorative edging around the soundhole and inside the binding around the body of the guitar. Narrow bands of marquetry, such as herringbone, are also commonly called purfling.

PYRAMID BRIDGE In the early 1850s, Martin began using a rectangular bridge with a small peak at each end. The raised portion had three flat sides (the fourth is slightly curved) resembling a pyramid.

RADIUSED FRETBOARD A fretboard with a side-to-side arch when viewed in cross-section. Most steel-string guitars have fretboards with a radius of about 14 inches. This means that if you removed the nut and looked at the end of the fretboard, the arc of the upper surface that you would see is a small section of a 28-inch circle.

RESONATOR GUITAR Also called resophonic, this style of guitar has a mechanical amplifying device that replaces the usual bridge/soundboard method of producing guitar tone. *See* Dobro *and* National

RESOPHONIC GUITAR *See* resonator guitar

ROSETTE The decoration around a guitar's soundhole.

ROUNDBACK Refers to the lute-style construction (stave-back) commonly seen on old mandolins (often called bowl-back). Since the arrival of Ovation guitars, the term *roundback* also refers to guitars with molded body construction.

ROUND-NECK *See* square-neck

SADDLE The lower bearing over which the strings pass before they are anchored in the bridge or tailpiece. In flattop guitars, the saddle is mounted in a saddle slot in the bridge itself.

SATIN FINISH *See* finish

SCALE LENGTH The distance from the nut to the saddle—the vibrating length of a string. Since the saddle on most guitars is compensated to correct for the sharping effect of pressing the string down to the fret, the most accurate way to measure the scale length is to double the distance from the nut to the 12th fret.

SCALLOPED An ineffective way to disguise potatoes, or a type of top brace characterized by peaks and valleys (scallops) that make the guitar's soundboard more flexible. Usually used on X-braced, flattop steel-string guitars. The style originated with C.F. Martin in the 1850s.

SETUP The work required to make a production guitar optimally playable. Also refers to adjustments necessary to make an instrument suitable for a particular individual or style of playing.

SHIM A thin piece of material placed under the nut or saddle, usually to raise the string action and prevent buzzing.

SLOTTED HEADSTOCK A type of peghead with two open slots. Tuning machines are mounted on the edges of the peghead, with string posts or rollers passing through the slots. This design is usually associated with classical guitars and 12-fret steel-string models derived from 19th-century styles, especially Martins.

SOLID WOOD *See* laminated wood

SOUNDBOARD The face or top of the guitar body where soundhole(s) and bridge are located. It can be either flat (classical guitars) or arched (jazz guitars).

SOUNDBOX Slang for the body of an acoustic guitar.

SOUNDHOLE An aperture in the top of the guitar. Generally either a round hole about four inches in diameter or two f-holes (actually shaped like elongated S's). *See* archtop

SPANISH GUITAR *See* Hawaiian guitar

SQUARE-NECK A Hawaiian guitar's deep, sometimes hollow neck with straight sides and flat back. Similar models had smaller, rounded necks suitable for standard playing and playing with a slide.

STEEL-STRING GUITAR A guitar built for steel treble strings and bass strings with a steel core. Not to be confused with the bass strings of a classical guitar, which are wound with metal alloy but do not have a steel core.

SUNBURST A type of finish, first popularized by Gibson, that is light-colored in the center and gradually fades to a dark brown or red at the edges.

TAILPIECE A string anchor, usually found on archtop instruments, consisting of a right-angle metal bracket fastened to the endblock of the guitar and extending over the soundboard toward the bridge. Today these are often made of wood.

TENOR GUITAR A four-string guitar with a short scale, originally tuned in fifths: C G D A (from low to high, like a tenor banjo). Many modern players tune them like the top four strings of a guitar: D G B E.

THINLINE A guitar with very shallow sides.

TIE BLOCK The raised rectangular portion of a classical guitar bridge located behind the saddle over which the strings are tied.

TRUSS ROD A type of neck reinforcement consisting of an adjustable steel rod embedded in the neck beneath the fretboard. The truss rod can be tightened to counteract string tension, thus keeping the neck straight. Access to the adjusting mechanism is usually through the soundhole or a slight cavity in the peghead just above the nut.

U-NECK The *U* refers to the shape, in cross-section, of the neck itself. If you cut through the neck at the first fret and looked at the end, would the shape remind you of a U or a V?

V-NECK *See* U-neck

VENETIAN CUTAWAY *See* cutaway

VOICING A part of the guitar-building process in which the top and top bracing are altered in an attempt to produce the desired balance between bass and treble.

VOLUTE A small shape carved at the back of the neck behind the nut. On Martin guitars the diamond-shaped volute was once part of an elaborate joint connecting the peghead to the neck itself. A curved, C-shape volute behind the nut, similar to the one found on violin necks, is sometimes called a hand stop.

WAIST The narrow portion of the guitar body between the upper and lower bouts.

WOLF TONE The tone created when the body of an instrument, or a part of it, vibrates and creates a pitch that is not in harmony with the note being played on the string(s) or obscures or amplifies certain overtones of the primary note. This is usually a phenomenon of bowed instruments, and the term is often misapplied to guitars.

X-BRACING *See* bracing

ZERO FRET A fret in the position where the nut is typically located. There is usually a nut behind the zero fret that determines string spacing, but the zero fret sets the string height.

How to Identify and Appraise Your Guitar

Teja Gerken

There are many reasons for determining the precise age of your used guitar. The most important one is probably pricing the instrument appropriately when you're looking to sell it. Prices for certain vintage models vary by thousands of dollars depending on whether it's a 1963, for example, or a 1964. You'll also need to know exactly what your guitar is worth for insurance purposes.

One of the most valuable and often overlooked resources to help you identify and appraise guitars is your local used instrument dealer. It's so important to establish a working relationship with these folks. While it may be tempting to call every store in the area in order to save a few dollars when you're shopping for something, developing a loyalty to one or two shops pays off when you need service that goes beyond a simple purchase. While most shops charge a fee for an official appraisal, it may take an experienced retailer only a second to realize that your old Epiphone is actually a Nova 390, produced from 1976 to 1980 in the company's short-lived Japanese factory. The shop employee may be glad to look up the approximate value of your ax in a book and give you an opinion about what it's worth. But if you randomly drop by a store that you've never been to before and ask for this kind of help, they might not take the time to look carefully at what you've got.

LEARNING THE HISTORY

If you want to educate yourself to identify guitars, the first step is to become familiar with the histories of some of the larger companies. In recent years, more and more books providing information on the major guitar manufacturers have become available, and they're a great place to start. There are some basic questions to ask. When did the company start building guitars? Where were the guitars manufactured? Did the company move in the course of its existence, and did it move its production overseas? Did the model in question change drastically during the years of production? For example, Gibson's J-200 started out with rosewood back and sides and fairly standard X-bracing in the late 1930s. It was changed to maple back and sides (except for a few rosewood examples) and a double-X bracing pattern in the '50s. Yet another double-X bracing pattern was used during the '70s, and then a more Martin-like scalloped X-bracing was adopted when the model was reintroduced in the late '80s. These are all differences that would be difficult for the uneducated eye to notice, yet they drastically affect the guitar's sound and value.

At the very least, these books will identify the time period during which the guitar in question was produced, basic information that will, for example, keep you from paying a premium for a "1960s Martin HD-28" (you'll know that this model wasn't introduced until 1976). Sometimes you can narrow down even further the time period in which

Three excellent books that can help you identify your guitar and get a ballpark idea of its current worth.

your guitar was built because of a certain distinguishing feature. For example, a volute or scroll at the back of a Gibson headstock usually indicates that the instrument was built between 1974 and 1981 (although some appeared as early as 1969).

Another thing that the trained eye will immediately be able to pick up on is whether an instrument was built in the U.S. or imported from one of the many low-end Asian manufacturers. When I worked in retail, a customer once walked in with a Ventura archtop for sale. Convinced that he had a guitar that was built in the U.S. in the '50s, he stormed out after I told him what I'd be able to offer him for it. Even if I hadn't known that Venturas were made in Japan during the '70s (which was confirmed by a quick look in the *Vintage Guitar Price Guide*), I knew as soon as he opened the case. It was mostly the guitar's thick finish that gave it away, complete with lacquered neck-to-body joints and drips through the f-holes. The wimpy hardware was another dead giveaway that this guitar was neither domestically made, as he thought, nor a high-quality import. The best place to gain this kind of familiarity is at your local music store's used-and-cheap section; the more guitars you inspect, the more experienced you'll be.

One of the biggest roadblocks in identifying a guitar can often be the serial number. These numbers are frequently inconsistent or missing from reference books. In many cases, a serial number by itself is about as useful as a phone number with a missing digit. Few companies have consistently used the same system of numbering during their entire existence (Martin is among those that have). For example, Gibson began using an eight-digit number in 1977. The first and fifth digits indicated the year of production (8XXX2XXX meant it was built in 1982). If you tried to apply this formula to a serial number on an older Gibson, or even a newer vintage reissue (which sometimes use "vintage" serial numbers) you'd be making a big mistake.

REFERENCE BOOKS

So, how *does* one go about accurately identifying a used instrument? Probably the publication most often referred to is *Gruhn's Guide to Vintage Guitars*. Written by George Gruhn (of Gruhn Guitars in Nashville) and Walter Carter, the guide is a must-have for identifying older American-made guitars. Organized into brands, general information, serial numbers, specific features, and model designations, the book identifies most major-brand guitars of the past and offers meticulous descriptions and a wealth of helpful photos. It offers little or no information on smaller makers, budget instrument makers, and recent entries into the guitar market.

Although designed to give approximate values for vintage instruments, the *Vintage Guitar Price Guide* is also quite useful in identifying instruments. While it doesn't describe each model's features in detail, it does provide a company history for most of the makers included. The book's many photos can be very helpful, and the general listings, which include many off-brands, are among the most complete available. As with all price guides, the dollar amounts shown are to be taken with a grain of salt, but having even a vague idea of an instrument's value will make you a more savvy buyer or seller.

Another excellent resource is the *Blue Book of Acoustic Guitars*. This hefty book probably represents the most complete compilation of information on guitars that have not yet reached vintage status. It's one of the few books that lists instruments made by companies such as Kay and J.B. Player and by individual luthiers such as Dave Maize and Steve Klein. Besides retail price information, the book includes brief descriptions of most companies and models listed, as well as a unique section on grading the condition of an instrument. In a color section, a variety of guitars are pictured front and back, showing a range of possible conditions—from 20 percent (poor) to 100 percent (new).

THE WEB

The Internet is also a useful resource for identifying and appraising used guitars. Although the Web is a constantly changing environment with more guitar-oriented sites appearing every day, there are a few sites that shouldn't be missed. Vintage guitar guru George Gruhn maintains www.gruhn.com, a site offering some of the information found in his book, listings of guitars currently for sale in his shop, as well as a good article on vintage guitar forgeries. Owners of Gibson guitars may want to surf over to www.gibson.com, which contains an excellent search feature. Just type in your instrument's serial and model number, and the site will (in most cases) provide a range of possible years of manufacture. If more information is needed to identify the instrument, the program will ask further questions to narrow down the possibilities. A Web site run by the Guitar Base Guitar Mall, www.gbase.com, offers a wealth of useful information, including a list of serial numbers for instruments by D'Angelico, D'Aquisto, Fender, Gibson, Gretsch, and Martin. Duck's Deluxe (www.ducksdeluxe.com) includes a page with guitar identification tools for several brands. And some small retail stores have useful information for dating guitars on their sites. A good example is Fred's Music Shop (www.fredsmusic.com), which includes a complete listing of Guild, Rickenbacker, and Paul Reed Smith serial numbers.

You can also join guitar-related newsgroups on the Internet, but beware of advice from uneducated participants posing as guitar experts. Of particular interest to acoustic guitarists are rec.music.makers.guitar.acoustic, rec.music.makers.guitar.jazz, and rec.music.classical.guitar. You might also check out rec.music.makers.guitar and alt.guitar.

These resources and the others listed on page 108 should help you on your way to becoming a guitar expert. All you need is hours and hours of paging through every available book on the subject, countless weekends spent at guitar shops and vintage instrument shows, a careful examination of all of your picking buddies' axes, and (let's face it) the purchase of a lemon or two.

Resources

BOOKS

Tony Bacon, *The Ultimate Guitar Book,* Knopf (1991).

Bob Benedetto, *Making an Archtop Guitar,* Centerstream/Hal Leonard (1994).

Bob Brozman, *The History and Artistry of National Resonator Instruments,* Centerstream/Hal Leonard (1993).

Walter Carter, *Epiphone: The Complete History,* Hal Leonard (1995).

Walter Carter, *Gibson: 100 Years of an American Icon,* General Publishing Group/Music Sales (1996).

Walter Carter, *The History of the Ovation Guitar,* Hal Leonard (1995).

William Cumpiano and Jonathan Natelson, *Guitarmaking: Tradition and Technology,* Chronicle (1993).

S.P. Fiestad, *Blue Book of Acoustic Guitars, Fifth Edition,* Blue Book Publications (1998).

Jim Fisch and L.B. Fred, *Epiphone: The House of Stathopoulo,* Amsco Publications (1996).

Bob Flexner, *Understanding Wood Finishing: How to Select and Apply the Right Finish,* Rodale (1996).

Alan Greenwood, *The Official Vintage Guitar Price Guide,* Vintage Guitar Books (1996).

George Gruhn and Walter Carter, *Acoustic Guitars and Other Fretted Instruments: A Photographic History,* Miller-Freeman Books (1993).

George Gruhn and Walter Carter, *Gruhn's Guide to Vintage Guitars, Second Edition,* GPI Books (1999).

Robert Hartman, *The Larsons' Creations: Guitars and Mandolins,* Centerstream/Hal Leonard (1996).

John Morrish, ed., *The Classical Guitar: A Complete History,* Miller-Freeman (1997).

Hans Moust, *The Guild Guitar Book,* Guitarchives Publications (1995).

José Romanillos, *Antonio de Torres: His Life and Work,* Bold Strummer (1987).

Robert Shaw, *Great Guitars,* Hugh Lauter Levin Associates (1997).

Irving Sloane, *Classic Guitar Construction,* Bold Strummer (1989).

Richard R. Smith, *Fender: The Sound Heard 'Round the World,* Garfish/Music Sales (1996).

Jim Washburn and Richard Johnston, *Martin Guitars: An Illustrated History,* Rodale Press (1997).

Tom Wheeler, *American Guitars: An Illustrated History,* Harper Perennial (1990).

Eldon Whitford, David Vinopal, and Dan Erlewine, *Gibson's Fabulous Flat-Top Guitars,* GPI Books (1994).

Michael Wright, *Guitar Stories, Volume One,* Vintage Guitar Books (1995).

PERIODICALS

Acoustic Guitar
String Letter Publishing
PO Box 767
San Anselmo, CA 94979
(800) 827-6837
www.acousticguitar.com

American Lutherie
Guild of American Luthiers (GAL)
8222 S. Park Ave.
Tacoma, WA 98408
(253) 472-7853
www.luth.org

Guitarmaker
Association of Stringed Instrument Artisans (ASIA)
1394 Stage Rd.
Richmond, VT 05477
(802) 434-5657
www.guitarmaker.org

WEB

www.frets.com. Frank Ford's site on guitar repair covers everything from changing strings to refinishing priceless vintage instruments. All with illustrative, high-quality photographs.

www.acousticguitar.com. Acoustic Guitar Central, the on-line arm of *Acoustic Guitar* magazine and String Letter Publishing. Includes articles, interviews, reviews, What They Play gear information from hundreds of professional players, a searchable manufacturer directory (with Web and e-mail links), hundreds of questions and answers focusing on guitar care and repair, on-line music lessons, and much more.

INSTRUMENT INSURERS

There are a number of companies in the United States that will insure guitars, and they can help you find the right policy. If you are not playing professionally, your guitar could also be covered under your renters' or homeowner policy, but be sure to check with your agent as coverage may be limited and probably won't cover damage or loss that occurs outside the home. Members of the American Federation of Musicians union can qualify for insurance services, including travel damage and loss. Here are some American companies that specialize in insuring musical instruments.

BMI Musical Instrument Insurance

J&H Marsh and McLennan
Arts and Entertainment Division
1166 Avenue of the Americas
New York, NY 10109-0218
(800) 358-8893
www.bmi.com/insurance
(BMI members only)

Clarion Associates Performing Arts Insurance

1711 New York Ave.
Huntington Station, NY 11746
(800) VIVALDI
(613) 423-2990
Fax (613) 423-2821
E-mail: clarion@villagenet.com
www.clarionins.com

Heritage Insurance Services

826 Bustleton Pike
Feasterville, PA 19053
(800) 289-8837
Fax (215) 322-5854

Merz-Huber Co.

630 Fairview Rd., Suite 200
Swarthmore, PA 19081
(610) 544-2323
Fax (610) 544-8286

Sterling and Sterling

161 Great Neck Rd.
Great Neck, NY 11021
(800) 767-7837
(516) 487-0300
Fax (516) 487-0372
(ASCAP or NY 802 members only)

Total Dollar Management Effort

325 Lexington Ave.
New York, NY 10016
(800) 962-5659
(212) 689-4477
Fax (212) 685-9268

ORGANIZATIONS

Association of Stringed Instrument Artisans (ASIA)

1394 Stage Rd.
Richmond, VT 05477
(802) 434-5657
www.guitarmaker.org
A group of guitar and violin makers that meets biannually to share techniques and information and to exhibit their instruments to the public. Publishers of the quarterly Guitarmaker.

Guild of American Luthiers (GAL)

8222 S. Park Ave.
Tacoma, WA 98408
(253) 472-7853
www.luth.org
A group of guitar makers that meets biannually to share techniques and information and to exhibit their instruments to the public. Publishers of the quarterly American Lutherie.

Guitar Foundation of America (GFA)

PO Box 1240
Claremont, CA 91711
(909) 624-7730
www.guitarfoundation.com
An organization for players and makers of classical guitars that meets annually, organizes a guitar teachers' registry and various newsgroups, and publishes Soundboard magazine.

SUPPLIERS

Duke of Pearl

18082 Greenhorn Rd.
Grass Valley, CA 95945
(530) 273-4116

Exotic Woods Co.

PO Box 532
Sicklerville, NJ 08081
(856) 728-6262
www.exoticwoods.com

Fossil Ivory King

PO Box 226
Seldovia, AK 99663
(907) 234-7870
Fax (907) 234-8001
www.fossilivory.com

Graph Tech Guitar Labs

PO Box 1794
Point Roberts, WA 98281
(604) 940-5353
Fax (604) 940-4961
www.graphtech.bc.ca

JLD Research and Development

2432 Lake Letta Dr.
Avon Park, FL 33825
(505) 622-3694
www.jldguitar.com

Luthiers Mercantile International

PO Box 774
Healdsburg, CA 95448-0774
(707) 433-1823
Fax (707) 433-8802
www.lmii.com

Stewart-MacDonald's Guitar Shop Supply

PO Box 900
Athens, OH 45701-0990
(800) 848-2273
Fax (614) 593-7922
www.stewmac.com

Timeless Instruments

PO Box 51
Tugaske, SK
Canada S0H 4B0
(888) 884-2753
timelessgtrs@sk.sympatico

Index

Other Titles from String Letter Publishing

 *All Include Audio CD*

Acoustic Guitar Lead and Melody Basics

The experts at *Acoustic Guitar* provide the fundamentals of playing leads in a variety of styles, so players can make a smooth transition from accompanist to soloist. *(64 pp., $14.95, Item #21695492, ISBN 1-890490-19-9)*

Acoustic Guitar Accompaniment Basics

For beginners as well as seasoned players looking to brush up on the basics, this in-depth CD lesson book provides the essentials of acoustic guitar accompaniment utilizing both fingerpicking and flatpicking techniques in a number of roots styles. *(60 pp., $14.95, Item #21695430, ISBN 1-890490-11-3)*

Classical Guitar Answer Book

In this expanded edition of *The Classical Guitar Answer Book,* virtuoso and head of the Juilliard School Guitar Department, Sharon Isbin, answers 50 essential questions about performing, practicing, choosing, and caring for your guitar. An absolute must for every classical guitar player. *(Book only, 84 pp., $14.95, Item #21330443, ISBN 1-890490-08-3)*

Flatpicking Guitar Essentials

If you love bluegrass and folk music, you'll enjoy using this popular guide to learn flatpicking backup styles, melodies, and leads. The outstanding lessons will inspire you to transcribe bluegrass solos, flatpick fiddle tunes, and add power to your solos. *(96 pp., $19.95, Item #21699174, ISBN 1-890490-07-5)*

Fingerstyle Guitar Essentials

Learn fingerstyle techniques, tunings, and arranging from some of the finest teachers around. This practical guide is packed with tips on fingerstyle accompaniment, arranging for solo guitar, single-note licks and double-stops, and playing 12-bar blues. *(96 pp., $19.95, Item #21699145, ISBN 1-890490-06-7)*

Swing Guitar Essentials

An introduction to diverse swing styles, pioneering players, and must-hear recordings. Learn movable jazz chords you can apply to hundreds of songs, swinging soloing techniques, jazz melody basics to use in your own arrangements, and lots more. *(80 pp., $19.95, Item #21699193, ISBN 1-890490-18-0)*

Roots and Blues Fingerstyle Guitar

A treasure trove of traditional American guitar styles by Steve James, one of today's leading roots-music performers, recording artists, and teachers. You'll be inspired and motivated by his clear, accessible arrangements and stories of such masters as Furry Lewis, Sam McGee, and Mance Lipscomb. *(96 pp., $19.95, Item #21699214, ISBN 1-890490-14-8)*

Acoustic Blues Guitar Essentials

Expand your repertoire with this engaging collection of ten great lessons on blues lead, fingerpicking, and slide techniques. Includes six full songs to play. *(80 pp., $19.95, Item #21699186, ISBN 1-890490-10-5)*

Fingerstyle Guitar Masterpieces

12 instrumental compositions and arrangements by today's best fingerstyle players. Hear all the original artist performances on the CD, and then use the clear, accurate transcriptions to bring their songs to life on your guitar. *(66 pp., $16.95, Item #21699222, ISBN 1-890490-13-X)*

For more information on books from String Letter Publishing, or to place an order, please call Music Dispatch at (800) 637-2852 , fax (414) 774-3259, or mail to Music Dispatch, PO Box 13920, Milwaukee, WI 53213. Visit String Letter Publishing on-line at www.stringletter.com.